Writers at Play

Making the Space for Adolescents to Balance Imagination and Craft

Mary Adler

Foreword by Elizabeth Quintero

Heinemann
Portsmouth, NH

Heinemann
361 Hanover Street
Portsmouth, NH 03801–3912
www.heinemann.com

Offices and agents throughout the world

Library of Congress Cataloging-in-Publication Data
Adler, Mary.
    Writers at play : making the space for adolescents to balance imagination and craft / Mary Adler.
        p. cm.
    Includes bibliographical references.
    ISBN-13: 978-0-325-02160-7
    ISBN-10: 0-325-02160-0
    1. Creative writing (Secondary education).   I. Title.
LB1631.A34378 2009
808′.0420712—dc22   2009017080

Editor: Wendy Murray
Production: Vicki Kasabian
Cover design: Lisa A. Fowler
Cover and interior photographs: Jessica Kam
Author photograph on back cover: Ben Hipple
Typesetting: House of Equations, Inc.
Manufacturing: Steve Bernier

Printed in the United States of America on acid-free paper
13   12   11   10   09   VP   1   2   3   4   5

Contents

For Bryan,
who has taught me so much about the play of imagination

Foreword

Years ago, I visited a mother of a four-year-old child in the Head Start classroom where I was participating while studying literacy in graduate school. I had developed a nice relationship with the child and I knew she loved to draw and paint, but I had never seen her make letters, let alone write her own name. I asked the mother about what Celi (not her real name) liked to do at home. "Oh, she plays with her older sisters all the time," the mother said. I asked whether they played one specific game or lots of different games. "Oh, almost always they play a pretend game of 'school.' Because Celi is the youngest, she likes to pretend that she is doing all the things her big sisters do at school. You know, because she is so little, she can't really do what they do at school, but she likes to pretend." I then turned to Celi and asked whether she did writing or reading at this pretend school. "No," she said, "I'm too little." So, I said, "Okay, well . . . would you take this tablet [the one I had been taking notes on] and just pretend to write like you do at 'school' while I finish talking to your mother?" "Okay," she said.

I continued to talk to the mother about family routines and the brothers and sisters for no more than three or four minutes. Then I looked over at Celi, and she had literally filled the entire page of the legal-sized tablet with writing. Most of the writing was recognizable as conventional forms of letters of the alphabet. And, right in the exact center she had written CELI GONZALEZ in bigger, almost perfect, letters.

Maybe she and her family thought she was "too little" for writing, but through play, story, and transformative action, she had become a writer (Quintero 2009).

I have learned that children are the consummate communicators, questioners, and listeners. They weave their webs of connection to others in their families, communities, and worlds. They don't live or grow in a vacuum, and they don't sit in school and "study" to be adults, with their attention only on what "will be" when they are adults. They are experts at being "in the moment." All children, from all backgrounds and histories, learn through their stories while engaging in play and other daily activities. They experience development in multiple domains and engage in multidimensional learning when given the opportunity and encouragement. Mary Adler argues that this is true for adolescents as well, in particular adolescent writers.

She says, "A writer must learn how to *play*. Here I draw intentionally upon children's play for its foundation, extending it upward to adolescence and outward to writing." Play allows learners to be autonomous and active in decision-making. Adler's research shows that her hypothesis was correct.

> Their intellectual, personal, *and* social growth are likely to flourish in the playful world of imagination. Within this world, rules are bent and reconfigured such that impossible ideas become possible. Within this world, writers are motivated and engaged in experimenting with and constructing an imaginary reality that responds to their needs.

She documents that young children develop executive control (Vygotsky 1978) through play, particularly make-believe. She says that if we follow this logic about the motivating challenges set up in play, and the opportunities to explore ideas beyond our capacity in the real world, we can see why this is such potential for growth. I would argue that young children, and adolescent fiction writers potentially, may move beyond executive control. The synthesis of executive control and creativity and risk-taking makes success on many levels possible.

I am continually in awe as I observe, study, and work with children. Particularly fascinating is the way they play and seem to intrinsically bring in their history, culture, languages, fantasies, and realities into every play activity they create. It should be common knowledge that play is important, but it isn't. Many researchers, most notably Vivian Gussin Paley, have shown that young children, through their play, construct tangible dispositions and skills needed for both social development and academic learning. Play elucidates perspectives of possibility.

I am thrilled to see that Adler cites research that clearly documents how young writers gain much from their focus on play, this "focused freedom" for adolescent writers. Adler's work gives teachers both the philosophical and foundational underpinnings as well as the specifics of how to implement this type of experience. In her research, she found that regardless of achievement levels, gender, or economic status, students proclaimed the importance of imaginative play in their lives. She noted that Sadie explained that writing fiction is "good; it's an outlet for my anger and my issues." Matthew said that fiction, as well as athletics, helped him cope with the anger he felt after his parents' divorce. Jack reported that he used fiction to rewrite his life in a positive way, noting that, "I am not a very agile person so I always dream about being very fast and very hero-ish. Like Indiana Jones or James Bond or something like that. I like to write about those guys or write about my own characters like that."

Simply put, students who learn to play as writers benefit from both the play and the writing—the push and the pull, as Adler describes it. Negotiating lived experiences produces more successful fiction and more developed selves. This premise is at the heart of this book.

This idea of learner/writer agency and more developed selves supports my own belief that all literacy is—or should be—critical literacy. This constructing of personal and communal meaning and taking action according to that meaning is the most authentic way to personalize literacy. Mary Adler's approach to creative writing relates directly to my commitment to a critical theory framework.

Critical literacy, stemming from critical theory, emphasizes participation through personal histories, sharing of multiple ways of knowing, and transformative action. According to Freire (1997), freedom can occur only when the oppressed reject the image of oppression "and replace it with autonomy and responsibility" (29). Freire felt that "the progressive educator must always be moving out on his or her own, continually reinventing me and reinventing what it means to be democratic in his or her own specific cultural and historical context" (308). According to Bakhtin (1986), language is intersubjective and social. Discourse always has a live meaning and direction. At the same time, meaning and communication imply community. Again, Mary Adler's approach to supporting, respecting, and enjoying young writers, in my opinion, is a pedagogical approach that reflects both critical theory and critical literacy. Her work gives young writers the space, opportunity, and freedom to create while they play and at the same time a safety net (or a bubble—with edges to contain the oxygen, as one of her students describes the phenomenon). They consider different realities, they dialogue, and they achieve transformative actions through their writing.

Adler is a big fan of adolescent writers and she supports their agency through encouraging play and responsibility. She notes that "the truly wonderful thing about teaching fiction writing is that teenagers also know how to play. They do it all the time—mostly quietly, even surreptitiously, when parents and teachers are not looking."

In the context of this brilliant frame for teaching fiction writers, Adler discusses and uses research from many sources to show different strategies for teaching writing and the varying effects of the different approaches. Also, she addresses the underlying nonnegotiable issue of what it is that "real" writers do. How do "real" writers exert their agency? How, through writing, can learners be supported in their agency?

Mary Adler articulates the duality and dilemma that most educators, especially literacy educators and writing instructors, face in these difficult times. She says,

> One voice intones, "Let's get serious—we must get our nation's youth equipped with basic literacy and communication skills to succeed in the workforce." Simultaneously, another whispers, "Hang on a minute—let's also cultivate

higher-level thinking in our students, equipping them to handle the kinds of imaginative problem solving they'll need to survive intellectually in our complex twenty-first-century world."

From where I stand, it is the second voice that is screaming at us to listen. My years of experience and research help me to be absolutely sure about this. Adler proposes, "Fiction writing in particular poses an elegant, efficient solution to the challenge of gaining *both* literacy skills and imaginative flexibility." In other words, literacy skills and play can, and must, go together. Mary Adler believes that

> What these students need is to find the payoff, to see how carefully selected details and events drawn from real experience give fiction breath and form. This is where our writers need help—not exclusively with exercises or formulas for stories, though these have their uses, but with instructional support that overtly addresses the relationship between the two worlds, the verisimilitude that grows out of well-anchored fiction.

Verisimilitude. Celi Gonzalez understood that at age four. Adolescent writers working with Mary Adler do too.

Elizabeth Quintero

Acknowledgments

From inception to completion, this book took nine years to write, and there are many to thank who offered tremendous support along the way. For purposes of anonymity, I am unable to thank by name the teachers and students who participated in the studies and provided immeasurable insight and wisdom into the writing and teaching processes. Their contribution is foundational to this book; it simply would not exist without them. My doctoral committee, Arthur N. Applebee, Judith Langer, and Stephen North, asked the hard questions and provided vital guidance to help propel my initial studies into a complete dissertation. I thank them particularly for helping me analyze creative writing instruction in ways that built upon prior research and theory yet respected the flexibility and spontaneity that the best creative writing experiences offer.

Colleagues in graduate school, particularly Eija Rougle, Steven Ostrowski, and Sheila Flihan, offered provocative conversations that pushed my thinking further, and Eija's reflective commentary on drafts, then and now, has helped me generate new perspectives on the material and sharpen my theoretical stance. I am also grateful to Nancy Dunlop for her poet's wisdom on the writing process.

In the past three years, I have received considerable support for this book from the faculty and administration at California State University Channel Islands. Faculty development grants, with the support of my chair, Jacquelyn Kilpatrick, have helped me free up time for writing and additional research. I came to rely upon the honest and immensely thoughtful feedback provided by my writing colleagues and friends, Bob Mayberry, Brad Monsma, John Guelcher, and Andrea Marzell. Without them this would be a much poorer text. Students in both my writing and teacher preparation classes read and discussed drafts of chapters and taught me about their learning.

Special thanks to Jessica Kam for her terrific photographs used on the cover and inside the book and to Ben Hipple for my picture on the back cover.

I owe a considerable debt to Wendy Murray, my editor at Heinemann, who shepherded me through the publication process and helped me remain focused on the needs of the teachers, thinkers, and writers who are my readers. My superb Heinemann production team provided dedication and insight, especially Vicki Kasabian, Renee Nicholls, and Stephanie Turner. Tom Newkirk offered astute and gracious commentary on an earlier draft; I took his advice to heart.

Finally, deep appreciation to family and friends who lived with this book, and put up with its author, for nearly a decade. Thanks to Jenn Wolfe, friend and teacher extraordinaire. Gratitude to Bryan for his insights as a writer and his caring as a partner; to my children, Lucy and Ethan, for teaching me how to invent, imagine, and play on a daily basis; and to their grandparents, Sue and John Benco, Jan and Ted Adler, and Constance Spiro, for being flexible, offering encouragement, and giving me time to write. Finally, to my late father, Dr. Robert Spiro, for the many conversations on divergent and convergent thinking: I treasure the memories.

Introduction

Playfulness, when the player's consciousness is fully operative, can be profound.
                    —Tom Robbins, in *Alive and Writing*

Let's begin with two questions: Why this book? Why now? We're in the midst of a high-stakes testing environment, with decreasing budgets and increasing challenges to education. As a nation, we have a lot to concern us. We hear the acronyms on the nightly news—the EPA, the SEC, our GDP. In education, NCLB and how well schools meet it—their AYP—make local headlines. In such a climate, writing a book on teaching creative writing—focusing particularly on the necessity for cultivating play within writing—feels somewhat schizophrenic. One voice intones, "Let's get serious—we must get our nation's youth equipped with basic literacy and communication skills to succeed in the workforce." Simultaneously, another whispers, "Hang on a minute—let's also cultivate higher-level thinking in our students, equipping them to handle the kinds of imaginative problem solving they'll need to survive intellectually in our complex twenty-first-century world."

Daniel Pink (2005), author of *A Whole New Mind*, would argue that this second voice foreshadows our entry into the Conceptual Age, a future in which "emotionally astute and creatively adroit people" will "survive and thrive" (2). By analyzing medical and corporate responses to a variety of right-brain-enhanced approaches, including the use of play and story, Pink forecasts a growing shift in favor of conceptual knowledge. In other words, that first voice is no longer enough. Comprehending information is necessary but not sufficient. Students today need to be flexible users of information who can connect, imagine, communicate, and reshape what they know and do. Enter that second voice. Enter creative writing.

Fiction writing in particular poses an elegant, efficient solution to the challenge of gaining *both* literacy skills and imaginative flexibility. In writing fiction, novice writers engage in a wonderfully complex experience: They develop imaginary characters, explore new perspectives, listen carefully to feedback, and examine what works in the texts of others. They compose lengthy texts, revise both in process and more formally afterward, and doubt and question all along the way. They play with remembered images and experiences drawn from experience, using them to breathe life into the text and motivate further exploration. Hence, we might say that young writers in the midst of fiction writing are hard at play.

It should not surprise us that while they are busy at play, these young writers are likely to gain more than the text of a short story. Their intellectual, personal, and social growth are likely to flourish in the playful world of imagination. Within this world, rules are bent and reconfigured such that impossible ideas become possible. Within this world, writers are motivated and engaged in experimenting with and constructing an imaginary reality that responds to their needs (Berk, Mann, and Ogan 2006; Bruner, Jolly, and Sylva 1976; Daiute 1990; Garvey 1976; Vygotsky 1978). While they do so, they engage in an astounding range of activities that influence their growth both as writers and as adolescents—ranging from abstract thinking (Chukovsky 1963; Vygotsky 1978) and problem solving to rethinking social and cultural relationships (Dyson 1989, 1993, 1997) to building what cognitive psychologists call executive function: the ability to focus on a task, gain self-control, hold and use information in working memory, and adapt to changes in thinking (Berk, Mann, and Ogan 2006; Blair and Razza 2007; Diamond, Barnett, Thomas, and Munro 2007; Diamond 2006; Golinkoff, Hirsch-Pasek, and Singer 2006). As Diamond and her colleagues (2007) put it, "although play is often thought frivolous, it may be essential" (1388). Let's take a closer look at some of these claims.

Abstract Thinking

Psychologists have long argued that play is a vehicle for abstract thinking. Think about the child who picks up a household broom, throws a leg over it, and makes it into a horse. This simple action has startling consequences in terms of development. Before the pint-sized Western rider mounted the improvised steed, the broom lived a purposeful life in the broom closet, its function restricted to sweeping the floor and perhaps a few cobwebs off the ceiling. Now it becomes a metaphor—an entry into adventure—released from its concrete meaning (Vygotsky 1978). Suddenly, the broom transforms into almost anything—a horse, a propeller, a flag, perhaps a scarecrow in an imaginary garden. The child discovers that meaning can be separated from the concrete objects themselves—and abstract thinking is born. If this example sounds old-fashioned, that is because premade riding ponies, called the "Plush Animated Stick Pony" at Amazon.com, have supplanted the need to create one from scratch. According to a recent history by Howard Chudacoff (2007), an increase in commercialized play products like these reduces the need to engage in valuable improvised play during childhood. This, in turn, reduces opportunities for abstract thinking.

As children grow into teenagers, the ability to engage—and desire to engage—in active, improvisational play may be less visible, but no less powerful, within the imaginative space of story. Here, too, adolescents manipulate their reality. Real-life sisters, brothers, friends, and neighbors can be changed in story into almost any kind of *character*, interacting within a new, fictional world. In story, our writers find a place to explore relationships, make characters act a certain way, and learn how that action influences others in the story. I argue that just as children grow developmentally from their play, adolescents grow from this ability to examine human interactions, to take multiple perspectives on a particular situation, to see events from an opposite point of view. These conceptual gains in thinking are particularly valuable during the teenage years, when relationships—and responsibilities—are multiplying exponentially.

In parallel with Chudacoff's findings on the reduction of play during childhood, opportunities to develop abstract thinking through play with fiction have similarly diminished in recent years. Even before No Child Left Behind stimulated increased concerns with test scores, National Association for Educational Progress (NAEP) assessments were demonstrating a "decreased emphasis on imaginative writing and an increased focus on academic forms in the secondary school, to the exclusion of almost all other forms of writing by eleventh grade" (Gentile, Martin-Rehrmann, and Kennedy 1995). The dramatic rise in national and state assessments in the past decade have marginalized imaginative writing further. As George Hillocks (2002) discovered, the increased focus on testing has often led to theories and approaches to teaching writing that contradict best practices, research, and national standards—all of which support extensive writing in multiple genres and drafts. For example, he found that the Illinois writing assessment rewarded formulaic writing while specifically excluding the genres of fiction, poetry, and drama. In interviews, Hillocks found that more than 70 percent of K–12 teachers in Illinois were consequently "hammering away at the five paragraph theme." This obsession with form—combined with a marked absence of creative writing—is part of a dangerous trend in the marginalization of imaginative, playful thinking and writing in K–12 education. Hillocks concludes that its exclusion "harms critical thinking in the curriculum" (203).

Problem Solving

In fiction, writers develop the kinds of problem-solving skills that have been shown to grow naturally in play. Think of the adolescent writer hard at play in a world of her own creation. While she composes, she *inhabits* that world (to borrow a term from Donald Murray, to whom we will return in Chapter 4). In some ways this is similar to what adults do when they become absorbed in a task that challenges their abilities and rewards their investment in time. Psychologist Mihalyi Csikszentmihayli (1979) calls this phenomenon *flow*: a space where one is so thoroughly engrossed in a task that time passes unnoticed. In such a space, *the immersion itself* supports increased learning. As Laura Berk and colleagues (2006) discovered, knowledge gained from that immersion in the imagination transfers back to the real world: "the more children engaged in make-believe, the more they talked to themselves to work out pretend characters' actions and to guide their thought and behavior during realistic tasks" (83). Adolescents engage in make-believe through the imaginary space of story, using it to figure out plot, dialogue, and conflict as well as problems emerging in real life, handed to characters to enact.

In the words of Jasper Neel (1988), a teacher of composition and rhetoric, students who play with writing—who take up the challenge to use language bravely in exploration of an idea—change in the process from a "finite, knowable 'self' into another text" (132). Each new "text" that emerges knows more about story, and people, and self than the previous one, because the act of writing, of play, helped the process of discovery along. The experience, as author Tom Robbins points out in the epigraph with which I opened this section, can be profound (McCaffery and Gregory 1987, 232).

Executive Control

Vygotsky (1978) theorized that play helps children learn to practice self-control and develop willpower. Recent research by cognitive psychologists supports these findings and recasts this concept as *executive function*. They also add that play helps children develop working memory and flexibility toward change. Recent studies have shown that executive function is a powerful construct, more closely associated with school readiness than IQ scores among entering kindergartners. As Diamond et al. 2007 explain, "Kindergarten teachers rank skills like self-discipline and attentional control as more critical for school readiness than content knowledge" (1387). The benefits of executive function do not end in kindergarten; rather, Diamond and her colleagues report that "working memory and inhibition independently predict math and reading scores in preschool through high school" (1387). Conversely, lower scores in executive function tend to be associated with learning difficulties including ADHD.

Young children develop executive control through play, particularly make-believe. If we follow Vygotsky's (1978) logic about the motivating challenges set up in play, and the opportunities to explore ideas beyond our capacity in the real world, we can see why it is such a force for growth. It is multisensory, using the full range of imagination as well as aural, visual, and tactile elements. It requires language, as children self-talk to help problem solve. Building on Vygotsky's work, Berk and colleagues (2006) found fantasy play to be the strongest influence on the development of private speech. This talking-it-out approach helps children develop the complex thinking required to control situations and resolve behaviors. Best of all, children refuse easy solutions. Rather, they "continually set challenges for themselves" (83). Given the depth of possibility for learning, growth, and control, it's little wonder that Berk and her colleagues declare that "imaginative play provides a firm foundation for all aspects of psychological development" (93).

It is a small leap from make-believe in childhood to story creation in adolescence. Can story creation also help develop executive function? Many of the conditions necessary to write good fiction also appear in Diamond's criteria for growth of executive control: "What you are looking for is a fun activity that requires sustained concentration, holding [often complex] information in mind and using it …and something that requires resisting what might be your first inclination" (interview with Valentine 2008, 5). As a reader, I am delighted to read a piece of fiction whose writer is having fun, concentrating, and testing out possibilities before leaping ahead with the next plot twist. Fiction develops best when the writer learns how to resist first inclinations in favor of what works for the developing, complex story.

In the next chapter, we'll look at optimal conditions for fictional play, arising *in the space between* having the most fun and imposing the most structure. In other words, it takes some balance. Fortunately for writing teachers, it turns out that what works for story development also works for human development. So we can simultaneously help students develop their fiction, and themselves, as they problem-solve, think critically, and exercise self-control.

Assumptions That Underlie This Book

Before you begin Chapter 1, which explores the way that play works in teaching fiction, let me articulate a few assumptions that resonate on nearly every page of this book.

Assumption 1: Student writers have much to say; their understandings help guide our practice. I'm interested in how writers talk about their practice. I find much to learn from the idiosyncratic strategies that students articulate—strategies that often are unrecognized in classrooms, but that these writers turn to for help. Throughout this book, I use these strategies, as well as other student contributions, including their drafts of fiction, interview comments, and journaling, to help guide and shape our path. I use them particularly in Chapter 1, to illustrate how students use and adapt to play, and in Chapter 3, to explore successful revision strategies. I draw not only from successful, high-achieving middle and high school students, but also from those who struggle to achieve. And I ask their teachers, as the classroom experts, for their feedback and recommendations.

Assumption 2: Professional writers also contribute; their reflections refine and shape practice. Hearing a published writer reflect on practice is valuable, but it requires a somewhat different kind of listening than we use with novice student writers. What works for Maya Angelou, who says she writes longhand on yellow pads on the bed in a rented hotel room, may not work for adolescent writers—yet these published writers represent the recognized best in the field. As such, they provide a valuable repository of experiences to us and in turn our students. They offer two "shades" of contribution, I've come to find. They offer exercises and perspectives on story elements, and in another light, when these writers reflect on their growth as writers and human beings, and the ups and downs of their lives, they contribute a vivid sense of the "being" of writer. As Tom Romano (2007) reminds us, it's good practice for writing teachers to "heed the behaviors of professional writers" (168). Such behaviors help student writers catch glimpses of their own future possible selves. I use these writers not as exemplars for students but as signposts along the journey, helping to refine our path and support us in practicing the art of writing *well*.

Assumption 3: Writing exercises are most helpful in context. There are numerous collections of creative writing exercises in the marketplace. And in Chapters 2 and 5, we'll explore particular exercises that are more and less effective, depending on how you use them. But my purpose extends beyond gathering a compilation of creative writing activities: Here I offer considerations for what kinds of exercises are most effective when and in what context. In Chapter 2, I set out several questions for you to consider as you evaluate any creative writing exercise to help you decide which activities to use with your students and curricula to meet your current needs. Later, in Chapter 5, I show ways to integrate writing exercises into a larger curriculum that is balanced with revision, unprompted writing, and reflective thinking.

Assumption 4: Unprompted writing is more valuable than writing exercises to your students in the long term. In doing the research that informs this book, I learned something counterintuitive about teaching creative writing: It's not the exercises that make the writer—it's the writing that makes the writer. Students need to function as writers, to learn how to create fiction that goes beyond the exercises. As writing teacher Penny Kittle (2008) puts it so well, "We assign topics and students respond by going-through-the-motions writing instead of from-the-heart writing that drives them to write well" (39). When students can avoid "going through the motions" and explore self-generated ideas, I've found that they inhabit the fiction more readily, make more substantive revisions, and draw more from real experiences. Supporting students in these efforts is the foundation for Chapter 4.

Finally, I want to thank you and support you in your quest to promote creative writing. Teachers are special kinds of writers, for they are writers with a pedagogical edge. There are writers who teach, and teachers who write. Both will find themselves in this book, for both sorts agree that adolescents need to write, too.

Exploring the Forces at Work During the Creative Writing Process

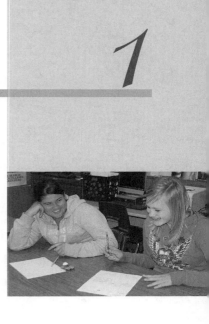

1

The agonies endured in math class act as great inspiration for poetic revelations.

—Kevyn, high school senior

One of the best explanations I've heard for how writing works, when it works well, came from a high school senior, Allison. (All student, teacher, and school names in this book are pseudonyms.) Allison, though fond of sprinkling words such as *random* and *like* throughout her conversation, was nonetheless completely serious about her writing. Even today, years after the pilot study in which I met her, I recall not so much her visual appearance—though that exuberant mop of curly red hair was memorable—as her earnest tone of voice. I recall her leaning toward me, elbow resting on the table, chin in hand. I could tell that she was thinking hard, as so many of the seniors I interviewed did when they tried to translate abstract ideas into language for themselves and for me to understand. In this segment Allison describes why she so admired a former writing teacher, one who dared to be different:

> My teacher from sophomore year—she would have us write papers, like quote unquote essays, in response to literature that we read. But she was like, I don't want you to just write a thesis paper. You can go different directions with it. You can do a found poem. You can do just a random poem. Or you can do stream of consciousness. And it was so cool! Because you could do anything that you wanted but it had to be bringing an idea to it. And it was freedom. But it was like focused freedom.

That one phrase, *focused freedom*, became for me a useful way to represent the complexity of interactions that happen during writing. As I finished the pilot study, all signs pointed to this phrase as an apt summary of the fiction writing process in particular. It fit the existing research nicely, and it fit with what I had seen and heard from numerous students who, like Allison, were thoughtful and serious in thinking about their writing experiences. And, indeed, it held up when I extended it to what I found in my subsequent study of creative writing classes drawn from four different high school classrooms in three schools in upstate New York (Adler 2001).

In all, my data included ninety-seven class observations, twenty-three student group interviews, eighteen student individual interviews, and sixteen teacher interviews. I also gathered student artifacts, 242 in all, that ranged from journal entries and homework assignments to poetry projects, memoirs, essays, and short fiction, including dialogues, character sketches, and full-length stories. Later, to increase the diversity of the pool of participants, I worked in my local community to test out some of the writing exercises with several classes of middle school students and their teachers. The high school study, combined with the local middle school project, form the core of the student and teacher material that I draw from throughout this book.

During my immersion in these creative writing classrooms, I came upon another phrase, ventured by Susan, who gave me a second metaphor to expand Allison's idea. We were in the midst of discussing an assignment in the students' creative writing class, in which their teacher, Matt Phillips, had asked them to write a decision story modeled after James Joyce's "Eveline." It was one of the few prompted pieces in the curriculum, so I was curious to see how students had responded to it. Susan's friend Nancy didn't much care for the assignment, claiming she "really had nothing to write about," but Susan said, "I like the way he gave us a heading and we could go kind of anywhere with it, but it was still some kind of bubble." Bubble? I wondered. "What do you mean a bubble?" I asked. As Susan thought out loud, struggling to find the language to explain this very visual metaphor, I began to picture her vision of a shimmering globe of air, providing needed oxygen—ideas, words, structure—for the writer but also acting as a barrier, sheltering the writer from all of the air in the universe:

Susan: A bubble is very, very, very thin outside, but it contains almost—there's so much that can be inside there but it's just like you're . . . it's a loose kind of assignment . . .

Mary: So do you look for a bubble? Is that a helpful thing?

Susan: Generally some sort of general direction that a teacher gives you to go in can be very helpful. It focuses your mind a little bit and then you can go from that. If you have nothing you don't even know where to start.

Mary: So the bubble is—metaphorically around you?

Susan: No. It's like—you have air everywhere and you have this one bubble, a pretty big bubble, which holds inside it certain air, specific air. There's a lot in there but it's not everything. So [when the teacher creates] the bubble, you have only so much to draw from.

Mary: So you prefer to . . . limit the amount of air you have?

Susan [*laughing*]: Exactly.

Both metaphors neatly capture a balance critical to productive creative writing: the necessity for freedom, open space (oxygen, if you will), and exploration—tempered and shaped by boundaries (bubbles, but porous ones) and limits. And now I'll add a third metaphor, one informed by a rich history of educational research and literary theory: A writer must learn how to *play*. Here I draw intentionally upon children's play for its foundation, extending it upward to adolescence and outward to writing.

Play: The Imaginary Universe

The writer, who needs freedom—air—to breathe in possibility, also needs a space in which to breathe that air. In writing fiction, especially, writers find this space in imagined worlds populated by characters of their own invention. Though these imaginary worlds invite play and exploration, the work of creating and maintaining them can be quite serious. As I suggested in the introduction, this process spurs developmental growth. Writers also engage in a different kind of play—play with language, as words tumble over each other toward meaning and possibility. This sort of play creates other, semantic possibilities, because it facilitates leaps in logic, spontaneity, and discovery. Throughout this book I'll refer to the two as *imaginative play* and *language play* (also called *linguistic play*).

Though *imaginative play* and *language play* are in some ways quite different, they come together during the act of writing fiction in a powerful way. Uncontained, both can be dangerous, leading writers astray, so they require some focus—a bubble containing the oxygen—to provide borders, even rules, within which the imaginative and language play can take shape. Both can lead to more productive prose and, arguably, increased writing proficiency in any genre. Let's explore motivations for both kinds of play and find out why these constructs are so powerful. Then let's look at the rules that give this play shape and make it function well. What we're after are ways to help students maximize the power of play in their writing—yet anticipate the need for control.

Maximizing the Power of Play

To understand the powerful relationship between a writer and the world of play, we must take a journey back to the roots of imaginative play—back to childhood. Why do children play? Educational researchers and psychologists agree on some basics: Play is a choice; it removes frustration; it stimulates pleasure; and it invites experimentation (Bruner, Jolly, and Sylva 1976; Daiute 1990; Garvey 1990; Hall 2000; Krischenblatt-Gimblett 1979; Paley 1991; Vygotsky 1978). In short, children play because they enjoy it.

Another reason why children love to play is because it allows them to be autonomous and active in decision making. Lev Vygotsky (1978) defines it in these terms: "The preschool child enters an imaginary, illusory world in which the unrealizable desires can be realized, and this world is what we call play" (93). Achieving the unrealizable is the stuff of fairy tales, genies, and magic lamps. Yet even small children do it constantly, altering roles to become mommies and daddies, police officers, villains, and superheroes. They change locations readily to blast off into space, climb into volcanoes, live among the dinosaurs, and fight space battles.

Although the imaginary world serves many purposes developmentally, Garvey (1990) notes that play, as opposed to work, "has no extrinsic goals. Its motivations are intrinsic and serve no other objectives" (4). Children do not set out to transcend a restricting reality. But the imaginary space in which impossible things become possible is part of the play world, perhaps its best feature. Play is a great way to negotiate the ongoing *can't*s and *mustn't*s of real life. As Rogoff (1990) explains, "It may be the *absence* of external control, the freedom to play with the rules themselves and to recast the goals of an activity from moment to moment, that is unique and valuable in peer interaction" (185–86).

Just a side step, now, to writing. In case studies of children in early elementary classrooms, Anne Haas Dyson (1989, 1993, 1997) looked at in-class narrative writing and performance. She found that children use play in their fiction—such as the writing and acting out of superhero stories—as an opportunity to negotiate and explore tensions in the class, in their home lives, and even in popular media. By varying plot, theme, and character, Dyson's young authors found ways to explore and even challenge the implicit rules governing gender, class, and race in their class culture. For example, a group of second graders wrestled with gender in conventional X-men stories (about a fictional superhero team) to such an extraordinary extent that one boy took to calling them the "X-*People*."

Moving out of childhood and into adolescence, we find that play is not left behind. On the contrary: Pretend play is simply more internalized, "projecting a *mental* representation onto the here and now, with knowledge, attitude, and intention" (Lillard 2001, 497, emphasis added). Sounds very much like writing. And adolescent writers live in a world rich with restrictions, a world ripe for imaginary play. On the cusp of independence, teens are almost, but not yet, legally able to drink, vote, move out, or decide where—and whether—to go to school. All of this becomes material, and the writing provides adolescents with ways to try out scenarios, test rules, and rehearse future selves. It also provides a medium—fiction—to reflect on the tumult of experiences and emotions that accompany these life changes.

In my study, I was surprised to find that regardless of achievement levels, gender, or economic status, students proclaimed the importance of imaginative play in their lives. Sadie, for instance, explained that writing fiction is "good; it's an outlet for my anger and my issues." Matthew observed that fiction, as well as athletics, helped him cope with the anger he felt after his parents' divorce. Jack said that he used fiction to rewrite his life in a positive way, noting that, "I am not a very agile person so I always dream about being very fast and very hero-ish. Like Indiana Jones or James Bond or something like that. I like to write about those guys or write about my own characters like that."

Janice also used fiction as the stuff of play, manufacturing a better reality. Feeling that her own life was "incredibly boring," Janice told me that she created characters so that she could "make [them] act *the way you wish they were*" at her high school. In the quote I selected to open this chapter, Kevyn cheekily described using writing to ease the pain of math class. Adolescents can, in story, even explore the moment when a boy asks a girl, "Will you go out with me?" as a middle school student does in Figure 1–1.

Taken together, these comments and written explorations are potent reminders that creative thought and play can serve as a rudder as adolescents navigate self-discovery, academically and beyond. When we don't give students time to do this in school, what might

The next day at school Sophie
said hi to steve and he told her
he had to ask her something after
schod. Sophie was so anxsious to know
what he was gonna ask her. Finally school
was over and Sophie was looking for
steve like crazy! So she dicided to wait
for steve outside of school, and when
she saw him walking up to her she
got more and more nervouse. Then he ask
her "Will you go out with me?". Sophie said
yes in a heart beat! She was the happ jest
girl in the world!!!! Steve was so happy
that she said yes and all he could think
was that he has the most beautiful
girlfriend in the world. Right away he
held her hand. Everyone was storing at

FIG. I–I *Excerpt from a story about teen romance*

be the cost to the development of self? It's a question worth asking as we ponder the long-term effects of a K–12 environment that increasingly limits the play of imagination.

Professional writers, knowing the advantages of play and having fewer constraints on time, are motivated to use the power of language as a medium, even a method, to uncover fresh understandings about the world (Arana 2003; McCaffrey 1996; McCaffrey and Gregory 1987; Murray 1989). Like children, they are willing, even eager, to see what can be accomplished in play. For adults, though, the goal is more extrinsic, more purposeful. Experienced with the interior world of the imagination, writers seek to use play as a method for *discovery*, a word that recurs frequently in author interviews. The late writer and writing instructor John Gardner (1984) reflected that "the fictional process forces the writer to say more than he thought he could; that is, to make discoveries" (67). And Phillip Pullman explains, "Anything that's any good has to be discovered in the process of writing it" (Rabinovitch 2003).

Both Gardner and Pullman recognize that imaginative writing is not simply a task of working out each element of the plot and then writing it down the way it was planned. Rather, they acknowledge and even seek out the unpredictable part of play—language play—to help them take their characters and plot to places they hadn't quite foreseen. Gardner, for example, advocates loose plotting of endings, to allow authors to remain open to where the story brings them and to take advantage of the discoveries they make along the way.

Less experienced writers have more trepidation with regard to language play. They know that as the text grows longer, it becomes more unwieldy. What begins as an essay on the importance of high school community service projects becomes sidetracked by the phrase *nursing home*, which triggers instead a retrospective piece about a pivotal conversation between an impressionable high school freshman and a ninety-six-year-old grandmother. Words lead to other words, extending outward in an endless play of language (Derrida 1978). Writers who do not plan in constructive ways allow linguistic play to take the reins. They may find themselves far from their starting point with no hope of getting home again. Yet those who attempt to shut down this play of words and meaning too early, such as by establishing a thorough outline of the topic in advance of writing, risk losing the generative benefits and unexpected insights—discoveries, even—triggered by such spontaneous associations.

The benefits of harnessing linguistic play are such that some writers even seek it out as a method for stronger prose. Peter Elbow (1998) teaches novice writers how to reap the fruits of language play through intentional free writing and deliberate, selective revision. By embracing the power of language to drag forth and articulate half-buried ideas from the subconscious, writers seek to discover textual connections, conceive alternate understandings, and forge new relationships between ideas. In the words of author Mark Leyner:

There is a certain point I arrive at when I have been gathering materials where I decide to enter a new stage. It's almost like I'm now entering the text, this information, bodily—I dive into it and begin to metabolize the stuff. I dance in it, play around in it, like I was in a pool. And then certain things start happening, I start to see certain relationships and rhetorical possibilities. (McCaffrey 1996, 232)

Lehner is an experienced writer using language play purposefully to come to new understandings about his text. He seems to relish the experience and to expect a growing clarity to come from messing around with language. The goal in this book is not to translate Lehner's experience capriciously into a class of thirty-five students poised to write their first fiction piece. Rather, let's use Lehner's words to capture a sense of the best that linguistic play offers, so that in curriculum planning we provide ways to allow some freedom, some opportunity for linguistic play to develop for our writers. In this planning, however, we also need to build in some focus, some boundaries for that freedom—helping our writers manage the inevitable play in productive ways.

Focused Freedom: Helping Students Balance Imagination with Craft

Remember Susan's metaphor of the bubble? It reflected her desire to carve a smaller, livable working space out of the vast expanse of breathable air available to the writer. Allison's metaphor—focused freedom, or "bringing an idea to it"—also implied a wish for some control over the shape of the assignment, perhaps curtailing language play in certain directions. Both of these limits are helpful to writers, because they go to the heart of the very foundation of how play works. Let's return to children's play one more time as a touchstone for understanding the process.

Watch a group of kindergartners charging around on a playground, and you could easily perceive an anarchic romp with mysterious rules that only the children seem to know. It turns out the rules are the secret to the play—it's not anarchy at all, but has cleverly embedded rules of behavior that give shape to the imaginary situation (Vygotsky 1978).

Even traditional games for infants, such as Peek-a-Boo, incorporate rule-based behavior:

> Each repetition of the game rests on the same sequence of moves, though certain variants in the execution of each move are permitted. What makes a good game of Peek-a-Boo is the mutual respect of each participant for the rules—that is, their shared expectations concerning what happens next and their willingness to conform to agreed-upon procedures. (Garvey 1990, 105)

Adolescents have clearly moved well beyond Peek-a-Boo, but their games of choice—texting or posting on MySpace, for example—flourish in part because the expectations are easy to define and each player can decide voluntarily to participate. See, for example, Figure 1–2, in which a student plays with language as a matter of course in an announcement in the school paper, writing in a code that only his peers are meant to understand.

Though research is pretty slim on adolescents' play with language and writing, we know that elementary-aged children who play with stories also make use of rules to help shape their writing. Daiute (1990) observed that children who were playing with alliteration and sound combinations were at the same time testing and learning the rules of story writing. She notes that even as the children were strengthening their basic knowledge of writing (phonemic rules), they were "exploring the rules of character description and development in stories" (40).

Similarly, Dyson's (1989) study of Jake's experiences in the early years of elementary school provides a good example of how even young children can negotiate rules to establish what is appropriate for the imaginary world of fiction—and also how notions of what is appropriate in fiction may differ. Jake was writing about his picture of a tiger jet on a mission to bomb a sand volcano in the desert. He encountered opposition from his friend Hawkeye, who exclaimed,

```
WHAZZUP4THACREW/
EXTENTIONSWALDZ/
SK8POPULARGUTH/TUESDAYS
WITHCMOKALLTHEGIRLSRYOURSPU
TZ/SHAMROCKPOWERWHEAT/
BAGCHIPSCANABUSHFATAL/
MM'SBIGLIPS4LYNZ/LOLSTEF/
CALLTHEZOOSEIZE/
COWGRLCOURTNEYGETSSK8BRD/
BESTGRLFRDAWARDKELZ/
STONIS!UH?/SK8FRDFOEVANICKY/
MOOSELOVEDAN/SOUTHSIDEJOSH/
ANUMERICSTYLECHU/
THUGLIFEFOEVAKRISTEN/AINT
THATAKICKINTHEHEADGENERAL/
FRESHMANSK8BRDERSKEEPITREAL/
YOUGUYSMADEITFUNXOXO//
PEACE.TONYHAWK
```

FIG. 1–2 *Student's coded announcement from school paper*

"That can't happen! Volcanoes are made out of rock, not sand!" As Dyson put it,

> [Jake's] text was being questioned in part because it didn't seem compatible with his picture; that is, according to Hawkeye, a bomb would have to be drawn well into the earth so that it could touch lava. As he saw it, the differing symbolic worlds did not comfortably mesh. Finally, the basis for argument was whether or not the imagined world was sensible, given their knowledge of the wider *experienced* world. (148)

In the end, the boys negotiated the rules of the game, finding a compromise between real and imaginary worlds.

What Hawkeye requires as a reader of Jake's story is what we would call *verisimilitude*—the creation of coherent details that help the story appear believable to the reader. In the words of John Gardner (1984), the writer of realistic stories "in effect argues the reader into acceptance" (22). As long as the reader accepts the details provided, the imaginary world holds together. The rules of the game apply and the play continues.

Though the rules of fiction may be endlessly adaptable, they nevertheless structure the play. Moreover, they make the play possible. The moment Hawkeye refuses to accept the details, the play stops and reality intrudes.

During my interviews with high school students, a boy named Michael thoughtfully demonstrated how verisimilitude works. He had just finished reading Raymond Carver's short story "What We Talk About When We Talk About Love." In effect, Carver had argued Michael into acceptance. Michael found one of the main characters so believable that he imagined him in the real world: "a real cocky kind of businessman [who] has khakis, and when he crosses his leg, his pants come up and you see the sock. He's drinking, and his wife is there. . . ." The realism that Carver created for this character enabled Michael to play along, too.

In my study, the opposite sometimes happened: Student writers had some particularly difficult moments when they failed to heed certain boundaries, ignoring rules that would have helped them craft effective and believable fictional worlds. Tim, for instance, completed an activity to develop a set of character traits for a detective in his mystery story. However, Tim and his friend Charlie became so caught up in developing Tim's character of a professor-turned-detective, they forgot about verisimilitude, ignoring their friend Donald's advice completely, as we can see in this exchange:

Tim: My guy can't do cartwheels—he's too fat. The person I have is a severe alcoholic, chain smoker, into prostitution . . . I don't know—cross-dresser?

Charlie: You've got so much there—he's a chain smoker, he's alcoholic, he's into prostitution, he's a cross-dresser—

Donald: You don't have to put any of this stuff into the story.

Charlie: You should though.

Tim: Yeah.

Later on, Tim's teacher, Gail Goodwin, came by and read his character sketch. Puzzled by the bizarre character, she said, "You've got to make him a real person." Tim, confused, offered to change the character, asking, "Should I get rid of just the professor? Make him a detective?" His teacher reasonably pointed out that even this change had to be considered in light of the whole character: "A detective? But if he's a detective, why is he a detective then?" Defeated, Tim looked down and mumbled, "I don't know." Unable to reimagine his character in the context of his teacher's request for realism, Tim dropped the story altogether. My analysis suggests that Tim's (and other students') difficulties in developing their mystery stories were at least partially due to the form and timing of the lengthy character development worksheet that we saw Tim discussing above—an assignment that encouraged students to play extensively in one area prior to an awareness of the rest of the story elements. In Chapter 3 we'll examine this assignment and others like it and consider when and how such preparation might be valuable for students.

Other students that I worked with also had difficulty balancing the demands of believability with the playful world of fiction. This was most striking during an assignment I call the Character Bags activity. To begin, the teacher, Jewel Fulton, presented groups of students with plastic bags each containing several objects, such as an old sweater, a tube of Bengay, a plastic horse, a rosary, a deck of cards. Next, she asked the students to use these objects as an inspiration to create characters for a story. After students created a character from looking at items in their bag, they were to trade bags with another group and create a new character with the new bag of objects, until each group had created five characters. Play was palpable as students picked up the items; laughter and curiosity rang out from every corner. Like Tim, however, some ignored the demands of verisimilitude. One group had so much fun developing their outlandish characters that they went beyond even the bounds of good taste. In the end, they were unable to write anything close to a believable story. The teacher gave their piece a zero, feeling that they were mocking the assignment. This occasioned lengthy and pivotal class discussions on how writers play—and how easy it is to become swept away in the moment, to lose sight of the craft, or art, of writing. For play to work, writers need to take control over their first impulse, holding it in mind while considering potential alternatives that may be more appropriate.

A second group in the class adhered closely to the rules, crafting a grandpa and a working mother that were as realistic and "normal" as possible. Indeed, one of their classmates noted that they did not seem to be "having fun with it." Another said she thought the characters would make "a pretty boring story." Their story was ultimately more successful than the first group's, and it was recognized in class particularly for good dialogue. Yet it was lacking some of the spirit of play. Even their teacher commented, in an interview, that "[students] all have grandpas, and they all have moms, and they know who's athletic . . . maybe they took those suggestions too literally from the things in the bag."

What I learned from observing and analyzing these occurrences is that teaching fiction writing successfully at the secondary level is a matter of helping students to achieve equilibrium. The creative writers in my study who were successful were those who had learned a specialized form of play, one that works within a set of self-imposed boundaries, providing enough room to entice the imagination yet curtailing play when needed and crafting it into viable fiction. Learning—and teaching—how to create and maintain this critical balance is pivotal, and one of the central goals of this book. For example, in Chapter 2 I discuss what happened when I restructured the Character Bags activity to make the balance between play and structure more explicit. When I taught the modified assignment to a group of diverse eighth graders, it proved to be highly motivating as a process, and it resulted in successful writing. Additional activities that strive toward equilibrium are also discussed in Chapter 2.

Language Play: A Second Balancing Act

The balance of structure and play applies to language play, too, increasing the complexity of creative writing further. As Flower and Hayes (1981) observed in their early yet foundational work on the writing process, the developing text itself poses additional constraints upon the writer. So does the process of translating meaning from ephemeral thoughts to words on a page. As Susan's teacher Matt

Phillips wistfully put it, the writer just wishes for "a language where there's nothing lost in the translation." That language doesn't exist, of course; rather, into that process of sketching ideas in text comes linguistic play. The writer finds that each word, linked to countless other words and meanings, strives to create its own coherence. Sometimes a battle for control ensues.

In an attempt to control the process before slippery word play has a chance to begin, novice writers in high school are frequently taught to organize their thoughts—to outline, to cluster—often before any real generation of ideas or thinking has taken place. This type of organization can help focus the writer on essentials such as character development and the arc of the plot. Yet as I discussed earlier, achieving the play itself may be the best virtue of writing—the place where the language seems to take over, each word leaping ahead to the next. In play we are in a pleasurable space of ideas where anything, for that brief moment, seems possible. Starting with the play, rather than the control, affirms the way that language works. As Jasper Neel (1988) recognizes, "Rather than a system for capturing thought (as if thought were some entity outside language that language, like a cage or container, could hold), entry into writing begins an adventure" (161). The key is to find ways to allow the adventure, while guiding the direction.

In short, a productive balance for both language and imaginative play can be illustrated this way:

$$\text{Freedom/exploration} \longleftrightarrow \text{PLAY} \longleftrightarrow \text{structure/rules}$$

When play works well, it's balanced between the concepts on either side: freedom and structure. When play becomes problematic, it's likely to have either too much freedom or an overload of structure. I explore variations on this balance in the chapters that follow, in the context of real students writing and learning in writing classrooms.

This kind of balance is new to many teachers and students because fiction is relatively rare in the secondary school curricula. Yet teachers should not shy away from it. Fiction is motivating. It affectively appeals to students who have been battered by the rules of writing without the freedom that makes up the other half of the equation. When we encourage adolescents to explore this newfound freedom through focused imaginative and linguistic play, we enable them to work within and across language. As they write through and beyond their own experiences, they gain new knowledge and perspective and learn how to pass it along to their readers and teachers. In Chapter 2, I explore the first steps in this direction: exercises for students to get the imaginative stories flowing by recognizing and taking advantage of play.

Exercises That Stimulate Play, Engage Students, and Build Technique

Finding the Balance to Create Productive Fictional Worlds

The genre of fiction poses a number of tacit expectations for the writer. The plot, character, and setting show us a story in such a way that we are willing to believe it approximates a reality; in the best stories, we are eager to move in. We want to remain in that house, revisiting its rooms again and again as we observe the details, witness the actions, and watch the characters interact and change. The rendering of plot, character, and setting makes use of techniques that help translate the writer's inspiration and spontaneous ideas into effective fiction. This is the art of the writer at work, sculpting and shaping the writer's play for both reader and writer. Often the shaping and sculpting come later, when the writer revisits writing and culls the good results from imaginative and language play. We'll explore this idea more in Chapter 3.

Yet writers also need to use their knowledge of technique to nurture the play, prior to or even during the initial writing. They might spend time just on character development or focus on authentic dialogue in a scene or try out different narrators or tones of voice. This focus tames the wild edges of the play, if you will, by directing its energy into particular areas. Learning technique, then, can help put to good use that explosion of playful imagination that infuses vivacity, color, rhythm, and humor into the language.

This chapter focuses on writing exercises to help students develop technique and story while they are at play. Exercises are standard fare for creative writing classes—this book would be incomplete without addressing them. However, I've found them to be most useful at two points in particular. First, they may help beginners develop some initial experience and engagement with the genre, as with the Character Bags exercise that I mentioned briefly in Chapter 1 and will explore in more detail here. Second, they help novice writers refine their technique, as with the scene and voice exercises we'll turn to toward the end of this chapter. In between these two points, *unprompted writing* is critical: writing that comes out of students' meaningful experiences and observations on the world, in which they locate the seed and watch it germinate. As Ralph Fletcher (1993) points out, exercises alone do not teach writing. Rather, "you learn to write by grappling with a real subject that truly matters to you" (4). In Chapter 4, we'll look at ways to help students identify real subjects that matter to them and to their readers—to find the next story, to "read the world" as material, to craft the real as fodder for fiction. For now, let's explore writing exercises as useful tools both to help writers get their feet wet and to help them develop and refine technique.

Considerations to Apply to Writing Exercises (and a Word About Soup)

One of my favorite cookbooks, *Vegetarian Cooking for Everyone* (Madison 1997), has a terrific chapter about soup. It includes great soup recipes, of course. But the really useful part is that the author, Deborah Madison, includes a section on soup *making*. That is, she describes the process for making vegetable soups yourself, even without a recipe. Madison points out, "Often we don't know why we perform [certain steps] or what they contribute to the process." She shows us what those steps mean and "why we do them" (199). This approach helps the cook understand soup in a flexible way, as a series of processes with particular purposes for each step and ingredient.

It's liberating to be freed from a single cookbook and empowering to have some guidelines to apply—or to be able to adjust a recipe successfully for particular diets or tastes. I take a similar approach here. First, we will look at three considerations that can be applied to any creative writing exercise to help ensure a productive balance between play, technique, and student needs. Then we'll explore several exercises in light of those principles. Of course, you'll want to season to taste.

When selecting writing exercises, there are three factors to consider: *play*, *technique*, and *scaffolding*.

The Element of Play

Play allows students to engage their imaginations. When selecting an exercise, ask: How much wiggle room does the exercise provide for students to play—to use divergent thinking, to explore beyond the conventional? Are students given a reproduced set of blueprints to fill in, or is there opportunity to try out different possibilities, to create different rooms and see what they might look like?

The Element of Technique

Exercises should angle the play so that it transfers to techniques in writing and reading fiction. What does the exercise actually teach students about the genre? In a dialogue exercise, are students finished when they have done some playing with dialogue? Or are they playing with dialogue with an eye also turned toward revealing character? For instance, the following exercises don't have sufficient transfer to writing or reading fiction:

Playing with dialogue for its own sake

Using the five senses to describe a place

Role-playing an event

Pantomiming a secret word for the class to guess

In contrast, the following extensions of these exercises connect to writing and reading techniques:

Playing with dialogue *to develop character*

Using the senses *to describe a setting so that you can step into it as a writer, and help your characters (and readers) "live" in that place*

Role-playing an event *for the purpose of testing out possible plot points or testing character motivation*

Pantomiming a word for the class to guess *and then writing down the behaviors and actions that students used to show, not tell*

Discussions of technique do not always precede the exercise; they often develop in tandem with play, and sometimes they follow it as a form of reflection. Whenever they happen, what is critical is that they *do* happen. Leaving the playful activity behind with only tacit underpinnings of the writer's task wastes the potential of the exercise to provoke conscious learning that can be transferred to other writing tasks. Explicit discussions of how writers work are important to help novice writers learn the uses and purposes of particular exercises. For example, Figure 2–1 shows one student's notes after a class discussion in which his teacher, Matt Phillips, spelled out some uses for dialogue.

At the same time, focusing only on technique without room for the imagination to roam squashes the spirit of play and invention that makes fiction so motivating and exhilarating to write (and, often, to read). I was reminded of this recently when one restless eighth grader wistfully asked, after several skill-building exercises, "When are we going to do the fun stuff again?" Let's not go too far and make fiction writing all work and no play. Rather, we hope to use technique to steer the play a bit, letting our ship surge ahead on the breeze with the anchor up, but with the prow pointed toward a destination.

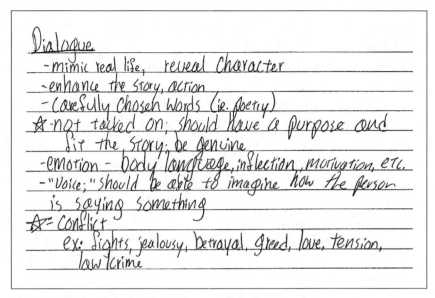

Dialogue
- mimic real life, reveal character
- enhance the story, action
- carefully chosen words (ie. poetry)
☆ - not tacked on; should have a purpose and fit the story; be genuine
- emotion - body language, inflection, motivation, etc.
- "voice;" should be able to imagine how the person is saying something
☆ = conflict
   ex: fights, jealousy, betrayal, greed, love, tension, law/crime

FIG. 2–1 *Student's notes about the uses of dialogue*

The Element of Scaffolding

The third consideration to apply to writing exercises is the need to scaffold the writers' play. One of the reasons why play is so powerful is that it gives the players a space—in this case, the story—to work with concepts and ideas that may be too complex to untangle in the real world. And play makes the complexity of these ideas into an inviting challenge. Vivian Paley (1991) puts it well in describing the story play of four-year-old children: "Images of good and evil, birth and death, parent and child, move in and out of the real and pretend. There is no small talk" (6). Adolescents in my project also played with complex topics, including politics, religion, sexuality, violence, television shows, and popular films. These topics appeared to be especially compelling for exploration in fiction because they are part of the real world these students will soon enter as independent adults.

However, the depth of interest in such issues and the rarity with which adolescents are allowed to explore them in school means that students who engage in this kind of play will need help if the results are to be taken seriously as fiction. Teachers must provide some support for the development of technique, as we have just discussed, and they must provide enough structure, in the form of scaffolding, to help students handle the complex literacy task of shaping a tangle of ideas and energy into a coherent narrative. In other words, because for many of our students the task of writing in general is difficult, and the task of writing fiction in particular is fairly new, they need to take it in steps, with support from teachers along the way. Teachers must create the steps of the process and provide the scaffolds. At first, you'll need more of them; later, once students become more experienced, some can drop away.

What does this mean for teachers in terms of the creative writing classroom? It means rather than selecting writing activities as though students are familiar with the genre, we have to apply our considerations:

Consideration 1: Does it help adolescents learn how to play appropriately?

Consideration 2: Does it teach them how to apply a technique or skill that writers use?

Consideration 3: Does it scaffold students' efforts?

Consider the massive amount of information a student must hold in working memory to write a story *without* scaffolding:

- Details of characters as individual and in relationships
- Setting
- Ongoing conflicts in a growing plot
- Potential scenes (in which details of character, setting, and plot interact)

- A satisfying ending

- Usage of literary elements and devices such as flashbacks

- Dialogue

Changes in most of these elements may change the story's direction. Now add information that should be part of the writer's long-term memory, but may not be:

- Relevant background knowledge for the story's topics

- Awareness of examples in the genre

- A precise and varied word bank

- Sentence construction ability

- Correct usage

It's not surprising that when teachers offer scaffolding that is targeted to support some of these needs, the writing experience becomes much more successful.

We'll look at specific examples of scaffolding in the second half of the chapter. But scaffolding depends on your particular students and their needs. The following questions may help you identify how many extra supports you want to provide:

- *What can my student writers do well with regard to fiction?* Recognizing what students can do already, such as writing dialogue, paragraphing, or selecting strong verbs, will help you build on their strengths. For example, let's imagine that last week my students successfully prepared a reader's theatre skit, pulling dialogue out of a short story to present as a play. I could ask them to reflect back on that activity through a quickwrite in which they jot down what they learned about the characters from their dialogue. I would expect that students would describe both obvious and inferential character traits as well as insight into the relationship among the characters. Building on students' observations, I might then ask them to try the following exercise suggested by John Gardner (1984): "Write a dialogue in which each of the two characters has a secret. Do not reveal the secret but make the reader intuit it" (204).

As we work through this exercise, students learn in a different way—by writing their own fictional scene—about how dialogue reveals character. In figuring out what their characters will say, these writers must consider what secrets their characters are hiding and why (and how) they would be hiding them. Students have already played with dialogue verbally and reflected on its potential to reveal much beneath the surface; these experiences help reduce the intimidation of such a lesson and increase the likelihood that it will be successful.

- *What help will they need on this assignment?* Sometimes I can see what help students need by circulating and helping them in class. At other times I simply give students an index card and ask them to jot down two things they know they'll need help with in writing a story. I collect the cards as students leave (their "tickets out") and use them to fashion one or two extra supports as needed. For example, sometimes students—from middle school to college level—say they need help introducing dialogue into a scene. Other areas that typically need support are using descriptive language, figuring out plot, and making dialogue sound realistic. Examples of instructional supports for fiction writing are listed in Figure 2–2.

- *What steps or supports do I need to add to provide this particular help?* See what you can add—visually or with graphic organizers, lists, discussions, or models—to help shore up students' weaknesses and give them the confidence to proceed. For descriptive language, I might have students brainstorm a word bank of vocabulary or use a cluster map for descriptive adjectives. For example, middle schoolers writing Halloween stories benefit from generating a list of words that describe sounds (*creak, groan, snap, thud*), sensations (*prickly, rough, jagged, gelatinous, pulpy, damp*), and images (*radiance, soot, crimson, rust, shadow*). Doing this as

Instructional Supports	Pedagogical Purpose
Offer realia (Items to touch and feel)	Engage students; draw in kinesthetic learners; stimulate the imagination. Give tacit permission to play.
Think-Pair-Share	Allow time for prewriting discussion; invite social learning; encourage exploration and play.
Graphic organizer	Provide a tangible support to return to during writing. Teach how to transfer the play to a writing technique.
Teacher modeling, large group	Model brainstorming and show how decisions are made.
Practice, small group	Encourage students to take ownership; allow them to practice the decision-making process.
Explicit reflection on the assignment	Revisit assignment in light of student learning; make corrections as needed.
Choice of sentence starters, if needed	Help students take the first step to imagining their story.
Initial quickwrite of first few paragraphs	Limit the air in the bubble; make the task attainable in small steps.
Teacher feedback (on sticky notes)	Motivate continued growth of the story; ask questions to provoke further thinking; avoid marking up developing story.
Whole-class explicit discussion of technique	Revisit the purpose of the activity thus far; consider what was learned about writing.
Student modeling of particular skills/techniques	Provide concrete, attainable examples.
Extended time to compose without interruption once momentum has begun	Allow time for the writer to enter and remain within the imaginary world.

FIG. 2–2 *Instructional scaffolding for fiction writing*

a group helps warm writers up and can also provide fodder for good discussions about overused elements, or clichés. Sometimes supports—such as techniques for plot development—are best provided at a midpoint or even after the initial writing is completed; we'll take up the timing issue in Chapter 3.

In a Nutshell: What Works in Creative Writing Exercises

- *Make use of play.* Play offers students a chance to work hard while having fun. Playful exercises stimulate invention and insight while motivating students to continue in their writing.

- *Include explicit guidance, before or after.* This guidance should detail both the purpose of the exercise and how to use the activity to develop or refine a certain technique needed in fiction. Both of these points help students see the playful activity as goal-directed; that is, they see a reason beyond the play itself for what they are doing. They're more likely to produce useful writing material, and less likely to get silly and unproductive.

- *Offer guidance on behavior and purpose.* Don't be dissuaded by initially awkward or overexuberant students. Adolescents rarely are offered the chance to play imaginatively in school; therefore, they will need to think about how to do so appropriately and how to play in ways that will support their writing needs.

- *Break the exercise down into writing components that may require support.* In Chapter 5, we'll look at how this works in the context of a whole creative writing curriculum. Figure 2–2 describes several kinds of instructional support that are essential to support student learning during specific exercises. These range from individual scaffolds (graphic organizers) to partner work (individually think, then pair up, then share) to small- and large-group discussions. It's especially important to remember to remove scaffolds once students no longer need them. For example, it is unlikely that you will need to provide sentence starters more than a few times.

- *Ask students to reflect on the activity.* At the activity's conclusion, invite students to revisit discussions of technique and other learning experiences taken from the exercise. Although some of these suggestions may not appear playful, help along the way allows students the opportunity to pick up the necessary tools that writers use to play effectively with language.

These approaches are highlighted in the specific writing exercises that follow.

The Character Bags Activity

Good for: when you're beginning to teach fiction writing to students who are just learning the basics of storylines

The Character Bags activity might be most useful early in a writing class, when students are still learning about story and need help in thinking about basic elements such as character development. This activity was briefly described in Chapter 1 as an example of unsuccessful play—that is, play that was not evenly balanced by the implied rules of verisimilitude. Let's explore it here as a case study of a writing exercise, looking at specific examples to help apply the three considerations I raised earlier: *play*, *technique*, and *scaffolding*.

I first encountered this kind of activity in anecdotal teacher articles, where it was touted as a good way to get kids thinking about character. Then, I observed it enacted twice in two years with suburban high school seniors by the same teacher, Jewel Fulton. (The examples I use here are drawn primarily from the second year.) Finally, I revised the exercise and enacted it a third time with a group of diverse, heterogeneously grouped eighth graders, eliciting their feedback along the way. As with all the exercises in this book, it is equally appropriate for students in grades six and up.

Ms. Fulton began the activity on a Monday afternoon in spring, when she walked to the front of the room, plunked five grocery bags onto the desk, and told students that they would be spending the period creating characters from the objects in each bag. The purpose, she announced, was "a reverse of characterization, where you read a story and determine who a character is—from what they say, what others say about them, what they do, and their appearance." She asked students to work in one of five groups, trading their bag for another group's bag as they finished. In each group, one student would record notes on each character as they worked.

Students pulled out objects such as an old sweater, a tube of liniment, a plastic horse, and a beaded rosary. They quickly began brainstorming aloud. The pace was lightning fast, the laughter loud, the physical excitement palpable. One student put on the old green woolen sweater and paraded around for his group, as Ms. Fulton shook her head in wonder. Another picked up the plastic horse and made it prance back and forth on the table as she talked. In a way, these high school seniors played like five-year-olds, readily inventing characters and their worlds. Some self-edited, but many did not. The next day, Ms. Fulton asked students to take their five characters and, working as a group, weave them into a unified story.

As one might imagine, the dramatic play that occurred during these first two days offered formative moments in the construction of the stories, which reflected some of the problems that surfaced during the play. Some students entertained themselves with outrageous characters, producing a superficial story with, as Ms. Fulton put it, pure "shock value"; others cut their more interesting ideas in favor of the conventional, creating suburban stereotypes. Roxanne, who had been the recorder of a highly entertaining group, explained that the problem related to the level of excitement and pacing: "And so many people are saying things at once, and it would keep changing. . . . So, I mean, it's hard." Her classmate Brad commented on how difficult it was to focus on the task "with this type of energy" going on in the group. And group member Darla explained, "The things that we were looking at were just funny to us. They were just funny so we went with it. But we weren't trying to disrespect the assignment and not put effort into it."

Although this exercise was not completely successful in either year, the rich potential for dramatic play intrigued me. The activity had been highly effective in deeply and immediately motivating students—not an easy task with seniors who spent their school time eating microwave popcorn, gazing longingly out the windows, and daydreaming about graduation and summer vacation. These seniors engaged in the activity—instantly—with an atmosphere of creativity and invention. Such potential should not be lightly discarded.

Let's examine the activity in light of the three considerations for a successful exercise.

Consideration 1: Play. Clearly, this is a strength of the assignment, which is immediately engaging to a wide range of students. And the objects in the bags provide a wonderful, tactile opportunity for students to explore a range of personal characteristics and experiences for each character.

Consideration 2: Technique. Here is the most obvious problem. The activity needs to be framed for students so they understand their purpose in crafting the characters—to think ahead somewhat to the goal of using these individuals in a piece of fiction. The exercise does have a strong relationship to technique because it provides a useful strategy to help students develop a multidimensional character. It is a variant on the typical "tell me what you know about your character" assignment in which writers receive a number of questions to answer (see, for example, Laurie Halse Anderson's "Interview with a character" activity at http://halseanderson .livejournal.com/201036.html). For the Character Bags activity, some discussion needs to precede the play.

Consideration 3: Scaffolding. Two elements of the assignment make it especially challenging in terms of student writing abilities: the large number of characters (five) to develop and then work together into a short story, and the difficult task of writing a coherent story in a group.

The revised project was surprisingly successful when I tried it with a group of eighth graders. I began by modeling—pulling items out of a bag, including a picture of the Eiffel Tower, a Las Vegas poker chip, and a hat labeled, "The Queen of Everything." "What if I found these in a bag left behind on a park bench?" I asked. I wondered aloud what kind of person owned these items. I gave students a graphic organizer and asked them to do a pair-share about four sides of our mystery character: her thoughts, what others say about her, her appearance, and her actions. (See the completed example in Figure 2–3.) These are the same issues that Ms. Fulton had mentioned to her seniors; I simply translated them into a graphic organizer as a tangible support for students as they went along.

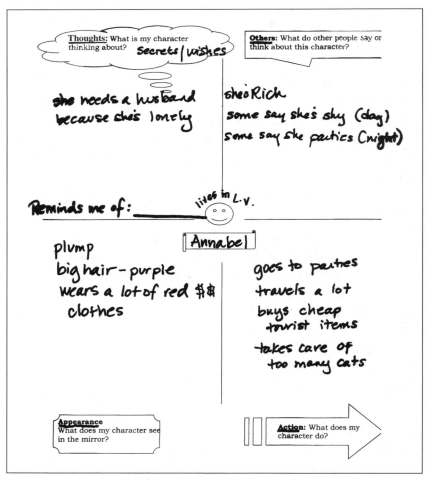

FIG. 2–3 *Graphic organizer for Character Bags activity*

Students shared their ideas in pairs (a low-anxiety way to begin imaginative play) and then I asked them to share some ideas aloud. As we talked about the sample character, I jotted down ideas on the graphic organizer, using an overhead projector. Students came up with some obvious characteristics right away—it's a woman, she travels a lot, she's rich. Then one girl delved beneath the surface and announced, "She lives two lives." Asked to explain, she said, "Some people say she's shy during the day. But other people say she parties at night." This student's certainty about the imaginary character's personality was a feature I've noted frequently during dramatic play. It may signify that the writer is fully invested in creating the character, who is, for that moment in that illusory space, a "real person." Another student added, "She needs a husband, because she's lonely." Slowly the students began building a character. They tested reality: Could she have purple hair? Could she be named Queenie? Could she have one hundred cats in her backyard? Such testing of ideas before using them in actual writing is critical to developing self-control. "Resisting what might be your first inclination" is one mechanism that stimulates such gains (Diamond 2006; Diamond et al. 2007).

So as a class, we considered each suggestion, accepting as many as were reasonable. We went ahead with the purple hair (some people do) but decided against *Queenie* as perhaps over-the-top. One student said she was fat, so we talked about respecting your character. I tend to agree with author Robert Olen Butler (2005) when he says, "As writers we must have compassion for all the characters we create" (135). Of course, some of the best characters in fiction have significant flaws or are even downright disturbing. However, it takes a skilled writer to navigate the humanity in such characters, to avoid stereotypes and shallow depictions. In addition, this particular middle school was wrestling with issues of respect on the playground and had recently implemented a yearlong peace curriculum, hoping to reduce name-calling and bullying. With both of these issues in mind, I asked students if they wanted to describe the character as "fat," or if they thought they could avoid stereotyping her as many would be tempted to do. After some fruitful discussion, they put *plump* down on the list. We talked about zoning laws for animals and decided upon "takes care of too many cats" instead of "one hundred cats." Periodically, we considered that students would have to write a story about this character in the end, and that, as I put it, "If you go too far in your playing with the character, you will have a hard time writing a story that makes sense."

As I added this upfront boundary, I wondered if it would inhibit play. How much structure was needed? I pulled out additional bags, each containing a different set of items, and sent the groups to work on one bag apiece. I also asked them each to take notes about their character on their graphic organizers. Having everyone jot down notes, I surmised, might slow the pacing just a bit.

As students worked—well, played—in their groups, I noticed that some did seem to go too far. Usually there was a voice in the group, mimicking mine from the modeling exercise, which tried to pull it back. For example, in a later interview, Taylor told me that Sam had wanted their character to be a blind pirate with an eye patch. As she reflected on this first day's experience, Taylor suggested that students shouldn't "go over the edge in [their] character creations." Alejandro agreed, saying, "Don't make the character so complicated." Because some students provided this moderation, Day 1 ended well. Figure 2–4 shows a character sketch of "Tiffany." This organizer reveals how the writers in the group worked through the process of developing characters with verisimilitude: The character is a blind girl with a Seeing Eye dog who nevertheless is a typical teenage girl, dealing with acne problems, loneliness, and feelings of homesickness for her family. (See Figure 2–4.)

Day 2 began with an explicit reflection on the assignment: What had been difficult on Day 1? Students had several suggestions. First, they felt that five items in a bag were too many, especially when one or two didn't seem to fit with the character they had developed so far. This made it hard to come to a group consensus with so many different and potentially conflicting ideas going around. We revised the activity on the spot and decided that students could put an item or two back in the bag if it was distracting. They could also jot down their own idea for the character even if the group did not want to use

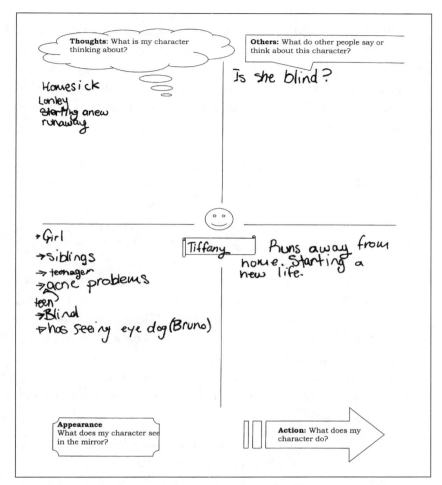

Thoughts: What is my character thinking about?

Homesick
Lonley
starting anew
runaway

Others: What do other people say or think about this character?

Is she blind?

Girl
siblings
teenager
acne problems
teen
Blind
has seeing eye dog (Bruno)

Tiffany

Runs away from home. Starting a new life.

Appearance
What does my character see in the mirror?

Action: What does my character do?

FIG. 2–4 *Character sketch of "Tiffany"*

it—or avoid writing down an idea if they disagreed. This seemed to free them from the challenge of group consensus and gave them a tool to make the constraints on the assignment more flexible. Then we repeated the exercise with a second set of bags, so they could develop ideas for a second character. The students readily completed the second character handout, along with much laughter and talk.

At this point each student had character descriptions in multiple dimensions for two characters. They were ready to move ahead. Although they had created the characters in small groups, I wanted them to write individually, using the group's characters and revising them as needed. In general, I've observed that writing fiction in groups can often be socially difficult, time-consuming, and counterproductive. (It can be done successfully, but that appears to be an exception to the rule.) I used the following scaffolding to help prepare them to enter their first story.

1. To begin, I gave each student a handout called "Creating My Story" (Figure 2–5). I asked students to summarize both characters at the top of the form: "My first character is _____. He or she wants _____" and "My second character is _____. He or she wants _____." I explained that this approach would help students summarize character motivation *and* establish possibilities for conflict between them. It also provides support for learning about expectations for fiction—arguably, that everything develops from the characters' deep-seated desire. As playwright John Guare (1992) explains, "The *need* [makes] the story. Creating the arc and completing it" (77). Some character combinations naturally created tension; other students needed to talk it out a bit before they figured out the relationship between their two "people."

2. Then, we brainstormed ideas for setting on the board. I suggested that the setting be both a familiar kind of place to the writer and an appropriate place for the characters. This support eases the cognitive burden of inventing a new setting at the same time as developing the other story elements. Students brainstormed a number of locations that they knew well, which would also fit their characters, including their school, their neighborhood, Las Vegas, a train station, Disneyland, a restaurant, and even the Summer 2008 Olympics (a student said he could imagine it, having been to Beijing, and one of his characters was an athlete).

3. Next, I invited students to start their first paragraph. It was clear that students felt ready: playful, excited, yet mindful of the story worlds they would be creating. I asked them to "put your two characters together in the setting that you've chosen."

Creating My Story

My first character is _____ . He or she wants _____ .
My second character is _____ . He or she wants _____ .

1. What setting will I use for my scene? I'll write some notes about it here:

2. Below I'll write my very first paragraph, where my two characters meet. When my first character meets my second character, what happens? Do they want the same things in life? Probably not. This is a good place to start writing.

In my first paragraph, I'll just get started with the two people meeting in the place I wrote about already[1]. I won't worry if it isn't perfect, because I can always change it later. Also, my characters might change from what my group decided—and that's okay!

---

[1] If (and only if) you are completely stuck, here are a few possible first lines (pick one):
It was a _____ day when (name of your character) ran inside the (name of the place) and demanded to know...   OR
(Name of your character) had never heard that sound before, but as (she or he) turned around in (name of the place), (she or he) knew exactly what it was...   OR
(Name of your character) had already decided (something) when (he or she) saw (someone or something) and changed (his or her) mind.

FIG. 2–5 *Handout: "Creating My Story"*

4. I provided three sample first sentences in a small footnote on the handout for students who needed a place to start (a "bubble," perhaps, to hold their ideas). Most who used the first sentences chose this one: "It was a _____ day when (name of your character) ran inside the (name of the place) and demanded to know . . ." Was this too much structure? Would it undermine the play? As it turned out, approximately a quarter of the students wanted to use the starter sentence, primarily English language learners who were more tentative at writing in English. That's the benefit about providing optional supports—when they are available but not required, students have the flexibility to use them only when needed.

The room slowly emptied of sound. This felt to me like the moment of truth. Minds were working, I was sure, as students thought about the two characters and how they would begin their stories. Angelina, a more experienced writer, asked if she could make up two new characters because she didn't like the ones her group had chosen. I said yes. Lilia told me she was having trouble because her group had chosen a silly name for their character, "Major Chief," borrowed from the popular Halo video game. With permission to rename the character, she went ahead with the story.

Offering students the flexibility to change characteristics such as names is pivotal to allowing room for play to develop. Students found that getting started was relatively easy once their first sentence was down. For most, one paragraph was achievable (see Figure 2–6). One student wrote only the first sentence, a handful wrote several paragraphs, and Annie wrote three pages. These are the kinds of variations to be expected in a heterogeneous classroom.

At the end of Day 2, I asked students to go home and think more about their story. I collected their story beginnings and took them home, where I read them through and wrote feedback on sticky notes. To provide students with scaffolding and a way to learn about technique, I offered each writer one specific connection to the story and one question or idea to follow up on. Depending on the skill of the writer, I wrote more or less. For example, in response to the piece shown in Figure 2–6, I wrote, "JQ, I'm very impressed that you

> Alsonso darted toward the path on Temple Avennez as fast as his legs would allow him to. As he was running, he was thinking about how different life would be now. He had just asked Sophie to the school dance, and to his utter shock, she agreed. But, he had other issues on his mind now, he was meeting his friends on world of Warcraft in 10 minutes for a massive raid, and after that, he had a planned session of team doubles on Halo 3 online with the only other person in Camarillo who could even match his skills.

> JR,
> I'm very impressed that you managed to reveal that Alfonso. is a geek without telling us directly. Well done! What's your next scene? The Warcraft game? Calling Sophie during Halo 3?

FIG. 2–6 *Story beginning and feedback*

managed to reveal that Alfonso is a geek without telling us directly. Well done! What's your next scene? The Warcraft game? Calling Sophie during Halo 3?" This question is typical of the feedback I offer students; at this stage in the story, students needed help pushing forward to the next plot point.

On Day 3, after praising students for the writing they had done, I decided to take the opportunity to insert a discussion of technique. Was the timing right? I didn't want to short-circuit the play. With high school students, more sustained writing time would probably have been beneficial, but the middle school students seemed to be at a point where they needed some guidance on how to shape their developing stories.

We began with a discussion about character development. I asked students to recall the graphic organizer from Day 1 and consider ways that writers help us learn about their characters. As students responded, we listed their ideas on the board: what characters look like (appearance), what they think or want (thoughts), what they do (actions), what others say about them, and what they themselves say (speech, dialogue). This overt examination set the stage for character development—the focus of the activity—but was hard to transfer directly into actual writing because it was abstract.

Next, we focused on concrete models. I asked several students to read their introductory paragraphs as good examples of character development. Niki's paragraph helped us see what her character looked like (she was wearing a business suit). I pointed out that this was the only story in the class that had described a character's physical appearance. This modeling was powerful; students later revised to insert descriptions on their own. See, for example, Vanessa's revisions to her first paragraph, including a note to herself to "describe what people are wearing or look like," in Figure 2–7.

JQ's paragraph showing how Alfonso was a geek offered a good example of what characters do—how actions reveal character. I asked JQ to tell the class about his goal in writing that paragraph, and he said, "I was really trying to make you see that he was a nerd without saying that he was a nerd." This was a nice example of showing not telling, arising naturally out of the student's work, and building on his prior knowledge.

To offer more scaffolding for the writing task, I asked Jeanna to copy a portion of her story onto an overhead transparency, because she had used a good deal of dialogue and had punctuated it perfectly. She read her story aloud to the class and then I asked her to explain how she had punctuated it. Because it was advanced, and I was curious, I asked her why she hadn't used dialogue tags.

"I don't like it when authors do that," she said, which surprised me.

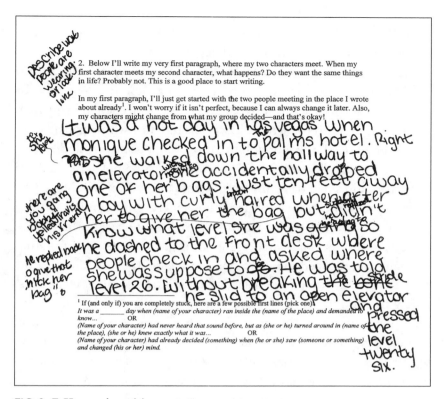

FIG. 2–7 *Vanessa's revisions*

"Why not?" I asked.

"Because it's obvious who's speaking," she said. "They don't need to keep saying *he said, she said*." I could tell that some students were surprised that authors had this sort of choice open to them. Jeanna's modeling turned out to be a useful way to incorporate some mechanics into the lesson for those who needed it; two students became newly proficient at punctuating dialogue as a result.

Then I asked students if they had any questions to ask before they returned to working on their story. Of course, I immediately encountered the timeless query: "How long does it need to be?"

"As long as it's in paragraphs," I said, "it could be two pages or seven—however long it needs to be." Seeing some quizzical looks about paragraphs, I put a sample up on the overhead and marked the indents in blue ink. "Why use paragraphs? What does a paragraph tell your reader?" I asked, somewhat rhetorically.

Matteo provided a lovely answer. "It's a new day," he said. Yes. In a story, a new paragraph might well be a new day—literally or metaphorically. While this support might not be needed in many high school classes, with these middle school students, whose papers were in desperate need of paragraphing, it proved a useful reminder.

At this point all of the formal instruction was completed—perhaps twenty minutes had passed. I set students loose to move ahead with their story. Now, suddenly, I felt a new energy and commitment in the room. Students were inspired—perhaps by hearing their classmates' stories. As I circulated in the room, I saw many incorporating dialogue. Some asked to put Jeanna's model on their desk to see how to punctuate it. Some were inserting descriptions of their characters. A few had trashed their opening paragraph and were starting over, incorporating description from the outset, which for the most part seemed a good move. Students seemed to like the sticky notes, moving them onto their desk for placeholding and talking with me about what certain comments meant, a sign that they were invested.

From this point, with characters fleshed out, the seeds of a story started, and an underlying reminder to describe what they saw, I wanted students to just write, in class and later, at home. I wanted students to concentrate on writing fast enough to let the dramatic and linguistic play take over as the writers "enter the text . . . getting down what we are seeing and hearing and observing and, yes, experiencing" (Murray 1989). Later, they could return to the completed story and read and revise.

The completed stories, when I picked them up from the classroom teacher the next week, were more elaborated and detailed than either the teacher or I had expected. After completing a first draft by hand and peer conferencing, students revised a second draft to hand in. Most of the students had typed this final draft; those without home computers had access to a few in the classroom. The teacher emailed me in celebration, noting, "Some of the students put A LOT of effort into this assignment. Yeah!" In addition to effort, the stories show students who were able to play with fiction, supporting imag-

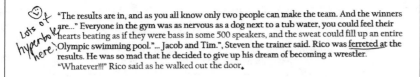

"The results are in, and as you all know only two people can make the team. And the winners are..." Everyone in the gym was as nervous as a dog next to a tub water, you could feel their hearts beating as if they were bass in some 500 speakers, and the sweat could fill up an entire Olympic swimming pool."... Jacob and Tim.", Steven the trainer said. Rico was <u>ferreted</u> at the results. He was so mad that he decided to give up his dream of becoming a wrestler. "Whatever!!!" Rico said as he walked out the door.

Lots of hyperbole here!

FIG. 2–8 *Yesenia's story*

inative thinking. Figure 2–8 shows Yesenia's involvement in the dramatic play of her text, which is reflected in her use of humor and exaggeration to amplify her characters' nervous anticipation. Her teacher jotted compliments in the margins as he read; he found her use of creative description—in this case, hyperbole—to be an effective device.

JQ's completed story, in which the geeky Halo 3 player finds romance, gave its author a chance to reimagine a future in which, as his teacher put it, "There's hope for Alfonso the Geek!" (See Figure 2–9.)

Although it was more time-consuming and required more support, this version of the Character Bags exercise seemed worth the planning, particularly because students' early experiences with fiction writing are pivotal. Getting them engaged in the assignment, supporting their efforts, and encouraging them to start thinking like writers are critical goals, worthy of some extra investment. Starting with two characters who have conflicting wants is a tangible, non-threatening place to begin. Later, students will have more experience, and teachers can remove some of the supports, such as the character graphic organizer and discussions and models of punctuating dialogue. As Jeanna thoughtfully explained during a student interview, "Next time we won't have to use a bag—we can figure out who the characters are on our own, and imagine what could be in the bag." Elements such as plot can also be discussed later, as a natural result of the conflict, a way to explore the characters' growth. Chapter 3 looks more closely at plot planning as a strategy for managing play after some of the story environment has been fleshed out.

Alfonso the Geek

     Alfonso darted toward the path on Temple Avenue as fast as his legs would allow him to. As he was running, he was thinking about how different his life would be now. He had just asked the cutest girl in school to the school dance, and to his complete astonishment, she agreed! But, he had other issues on his mind now. He was meeting for a group raid on the Human Capitol city, Stormwind City, on World of Warcraft, and after that, he had a planned session of Halo 3 with the only person in Camarillo who could even possibly match his skill!   *← had agreed*

     "Okay guys, we need to take out these level 65's before we can assault the actual city." Alfonso said into the microphone, "or we'll never stand a chance and get attacked in groups."

     "Alfonso!!!!!!!!" An earsplitting scream came from his sister Jill's room, and she stormed into Alfonso's room, "Where's Mr. Ele?!?"

     "I don't know, check your animal chest, and I'm busy!" Alfonso shot at his sister spitefully.

     Jill dashed out of his room, and came back seconds later, with Mr. Ele in her arms.

     Alfonso looked up and it was 6:30, time to play Halo 3.

     The score was 24-24, one more kill and the game would be over. Alfonso kept his eyes glued on the radar, hoping one of his enemies would round the corner, the game was all his! He jumped from his hiding spot, tried to lunge for the enemy, but missed! Now he had two battle rifles on his head, but Alfonso's covenant soldier was skilled and fierce. He rushed toward the foolish Spartan, and kept trying to swipe at him, but the Spartan was very nimble.

     Just then, Alfonso's ringer went off, THE ringtone. Pure terror came over Alfonso. Suddenly he forgot about the Halo game, and rushed toward the phone.   *GREAT Nice change in tone! It's abrupt, and yet realistic*

     "Hello?" Alfonso managed to croak.

     "Hi, is Alfonso there?" replied a cool, confident voice.

     "Yes, it's me." He was gaining confidence now.

     "Umm...there is a slight problem, my parents said that I can't go to the dance." Complete silence fell over the line, "I'm really sorry, I really would like to go with you." Alfonso was devastated by the rejection. He knew that she was able to go, but she was using the 'parent' excuse. He knew she was just trying to spare his feelings.

FIG. 2–9 *JQ's completed story*

The other big lesson in this exercise was the importance of flexibility and listening to students' in-the-moment feedback on the assignment. Students in a differentiated classroom by definition have varying levels of proficiency with writing, and allowing some to depart from the script if they are ready, as Angelina did when she asked to develop her own characters apart from the group, helps to maintain engagement throughout.

Here are the steps for trying the Character Bags activity in your own classroom. You can drop or add supports as needed for your particular students.

Steps for the Character Bags Activity

1. Model character development. Use a sample bag, think-pair-share, and then whole-class discussion.

2. Model using a graphic organizer for character, as in Figure 2–3. Use the modeling discussion to set the purpose for the activity and demonstrate how to play appropriately.

3. Allow groups to complete the exercise with one or two bags. Circulate.

4. As a class, reflect on the activity and adjust areas of difficulty (e.g., allow flexibility in how many items are used and in how much consensus is needed).

5. Continue with another one or two bags.

6. Provide story scaffolding. Offer students a handout to develop characters and conflict. Keep it simple. See Figure 2–5 for some ideas.

7. Identify familiar settings students can use that are appropriate for their characters.

8. Assign the first writing activity (one paragraph or more depending on the class). Ask students to put two characters together in a setting and see what happens. Provide sample first sentences for ELL students or others who need support.

9. Circulate and remain flexible as students need support in developing individual concepts. Ask them questions to get ideas flowing.

10. Collect drafts and provide feedback on sticky notes. Limit feedback to one or two comments, questions, or suggestions.

11. Revisit the concept of characterization and return to student models for strong examples.

12. Provide models for other literacy skills as needed (punctuating dialogue, paragraphing, sentence variety, word choice, etc.).

13. Return drafts and ask for questions. Set aside a good chunk of writing time for students to move ahead to complete their drafts. Continue revising and editing as time permits.

Developing Scene

Good for: when students need help with showing not telling, developing scene rather than rushing through it

In addition to character development, another foundational element of fiction that is worthy of a writers' exercise is *scene*. Often, inexperienced writers, particularly when they are pressed for time, will summarize a scene without letting the reader experience it. For example, rather than showing us a scene in which a father and daughter have a final conversation, a writer out of time or inspiration might instead write the following: *Her father left when she was twelve. She hated him for leaving and walking away. She would never forget that day.* Although this synopsis gives us a plot point, we do not see the conversation or hear what the father and daughter said to one another. We do not see this interaction because the writer does not see the conversation. And both reader and writer lose a window of opportunity to learn about both characters.

Developing a scene helps writers avoid telling. Although they use only two ingredients—dialogue and narration—scenes offer writers a powerful boost to producing better fiction, in part because they help the reader observe the characters closely "in an unbroken flow of action from one incident in time to another" (Gardner 1984, 59). They are also likely to help raise the quality of the overall story. The National Assessment of Educational Progress (NAEP), which has assessed students in writing and other areas since 1969, defines a number of measures as being important to narrative, including those that help "integrate narrative events into a smooth telling" and "tell a clear story that is consistently well developed and detailed" (U.S. Department of Education 2003, 92). The NAEP emphasis on degree of development and detail as a prime criteria rewards those writers who know how to sustain a scene long enough to describe the action and characters. On the other hand, those who simply list events rather than describe actual scenes would be more likely to score in the "uneven" or "insufficient" range, producing fiction that is "minimally developed" or "list-like."

Learning how to create effective scenes, in short, is a technique useful for upping the quality of the whole. The writer begins to think of the story as a series of connected scenes, rather than as a list of events. As Gardner (1984) put it, an effective writer "makes each scene bear as much as it can without clutter or crowding and moves by the smoothest, swiftest transitions possible from scene to scene" (59).

In terms of imaginative play, writers need scene to help them, as Murray says, *inhabit* their story (more on this in Chapter 4). If they're going to live awhile in the house they're building, they need to sit at the table for breakfast, listen to their characters' voices, and see them walking, running, fighting, or ducking for cover.

The scene exercise is straightforward: Provide the dialogue and ask writers to transform it into a scene. I first encountered this exercise at the University of Iowa in 2005 during a summer writing workshop that was directed by B. K. Loren, and I immediately realized its tremendous usefulness. Since then, students ranging in age from middle school to college have told me the same. Like the Character Bags activity, it is simple and intuitive for students. Here are the four steps:

1. Give writers a dialogue, written loosely in play format, with the characters' names and all stage direction removed. When selecting dialogue, try to find a complete scene that is short, about eight to ten lines in total, that reveals some tension. I've had good luck finding scenes in screenplays online, or you can transcribe a short scene from a film you like. *The Karate Kid* and *The Breakfast Club* have some good tense moments that resonate with adolescents— and the films are old enough that most students will not recognize the dialogue, especially with characters' names removed.

2. Ask students to create a scene, using the characters' exact words as given. They may use their own paper or fill in the lines on the page between the dialogue. Encourage students to visualize the scene like a movie director—creating it, filming it, inhabiting it, making it their own, and adding gestures, description, setting, and sound—whatever is needed to bring it to life.

3. Have some writers share their scenes in small groups, then share as a whole class. In both situations, discuss the choices writers made: Which character did they sympathize with? How did they show their sympathy in the scene? How was character revealed, aside from dialogue? How did these choices change the way the reader interprets the dialogue? Also, consider plot: What came before this scene? What might come after? How do you know?

4. If you can, show the clip of the original scene as the film director and actors interpreted it and ask the students to comment on the visual, stylistic, and acting choices. As an optional extension, you may ask students to reflect in writing on what they've learned about writing a scene. Draw upon this knowledge again in a later class; the experience can serve as a touchstone for further discussion on scene, character, and plot.

Here's an example of what I did with the exercise when I first encountered it as a workshop participant. The workshop leader, B. K. Loren, presented the following dialogue, adapted from the shooting script of *You Can Count on Me* (Lonergan 2000):

MAN

So, are you just coming from work?

WOMAN

No—It's Saturday.

MAN

It's just—you're dressed so formally.

WOMAN

Oh, you know, I thought I'd get dressed up . . .
I thought it was a special occasion—which it is. . . .

MAN

It's good, no it's good. I thought I'd get dressed up, too.

WOMAN

You look fine.

MAN

Yeah, this is the haute cuisine of garments.

WOMAN

What?

Here's my take on the scene:

Jack saw her before she saw him. Standing, wearing a black
silk blouse, the kind that billows out a bit when it's tucked in,
and it was, into a red skirt that hung straight down her hips,
drawing his eyes to her black patent-leather high heels. He
buttoned up his flannel shirt and brushed his jeans down with
his fingertips before he opened one of the double glass doors
to the little Italian place she'd picked out the night before.

She turned and saw him watching her. Gave him a hug, a
cheek to kiss. Smiled up at him, and brushed some hair off his
forehead. He could see the soft polish on the clean, well-
shaped nails, the simple gold ring, the modest neckline. They
said their hellos and went to stand at the bar. He ordered a
whisky and Coke. She asked for a glass of Chablis. He'd never
known her to drink white wine.

"So, are you just coming from work?" he asked. He took a
drink. Light on the Coke, heavy on the whiskey.

"No—It's Saturday," she said, her hand resting on the back
of one of those velvet-backed barstools.

"It's just—you're dressed so formally."

"Oh, you know, I thought I'd get dressed up." She looked
up at him. He looked away, at the bartender, who caught his
eye, so he ordered another drink.

"I thought it was a special occasion—which it is. . . ." Her voice trailed off.

He straightened his collar and looked over at her. She was trying to smile, looking up at him, trying to get him to look at her.

"It's good, no it's good," he said. "I thought I'd get dressed up, too," he added.

"You look fine," she said.

"Yeah, this is the haute cuisine of garments." He reached for his second whiskey.

"What?"

As may be evident, I haven't yet figured out these two characters as individuals, though I've gotten a sense of the conflict between them. There is plenty of potential to take this somewhere else (and, writing exercises are most useful when they are authentic—when they can become a piece of one's own writing, more than just an exercise). I'd also share it with my class, for I agree with Penny Kittle's carefully reasoned argument for why teachers need to write alongside their students. As she explains, "We don't learn many things well just by following directions. We have to ride together" (2008, 7–8). I'd want to hear my students' ideas about this scene. And I'd want them to know that this is a first scene, a step into this story world, and that so far, this felt pretty good. But why did it work? Let's look at our three considerations for a successful exercise.

Play. Writers of all shapes and sizes appear to enjoy the challenge of crafting the dialogue into a scene. They have free rein to select any setting that works, create any characters that can fit the dialogue. The written lines on the page, with the tenuous coherence between them, provide the "rules" for the play. Yet there is flexibility in interpreting these "rules." A line can be playful, angry, solemn, sarcastic—the writer decides and interprets. The social nature of the activity, with others writing on the same dialogue and with the expectation of sharing different takes on the same scene, creates additional motivation.

Technique. The fact that the writer is building on an existing, coherent dialogue creates opportunities to learn about the shape of a scene and the tension that drives it. Indeed, the central goal of the activity is to find a way to *reveal* the tension embedded in the dialogue, to reveal feelings in the characters, without the use of additional speech. This forces writers to expand their use of description, setting, and especially character action, and it introduces the development of tone. After a group of eighth graders completed the exercise, they reflected on what they had learned, including their own take on elements of a writer's craft:

> One thing I have learned from the dialogue/narrative exercise is if two or more people are talking to each other you can tell their mood. (Josie)
>
> I learned that dialogue is good for a story but it takes narration to make sense of the story. (Michael)
>
> I learned that without direction or description, dialogue isn't very good. (Maria)
>
> Dialogue can show a character's demeanor. (Nick)
>
> It is really important to show a character's actions as well as their words. (Abby)

The discussion and comparison of the fleshed-out scenes help students articulate this learning and can be drawn on later during student writing and class discussions of literature.

Scaffolding. I like this exercise because it takes into consideration the large number of elements that a writer must attend to in creating a story—dialogue *and* narrative; character *and* plot; setting *and* scene. As a support for the student, it provides at least half of each of those equations. The dialogue is given, so the student only needs to work on the narrative. Plot and character are each hinted at, heavily (one perhaps more than the other, depending on the excerpt you've chosen), allowing the student to build on what is already there. Setting is missing, but there is enough of a scene to allow the writer to infer a probable location from the dialogue and go to work describing it from the ground up. Additionally, the metaphor of a director and a movie camera seems to help students understand their role as writers—they need to be the eyes of the camera for the audience, who has only the sound.

Students will learn at different levels, depending on their experience and needs. Using this exercise, a student named David finally figured out the mechanics of dialogue. This was a big aha moment for him. He explained, "I learned that when you do dialogue you don't put the dialogue side to side, you put it up and down. I also learned that you put [quotation marks] to make it dialogue."

Steps for the Dialogue-in-Scene Activity

1. Provide students with dialogue only from a short film or television script.

2. Read it aloud, then direct students to think like a director and turn it into a fiction scene. They use the dialogue as is, but add setting, character description, movement, body language, or other narration as needed.

3. Ask students to share their work in pairs or small groups and to discuss the following questions:
   - Which character did you feel closest to and sympathize with? How is it shown in the scene?
   - What decisions did you make as a writer and what was the effect of those decisions on the scene?
   - How did you reveal character?
   - What do you think might precede and/or follow this scene?

4. Discuss the scenes and questions with the whole class. When individual sharing is completed, ask the following question to extend students' thinking:
   - What makes a "scene" complete? How do you know?

5. If time permits, show the clip of the original scene and discuss directing choices. Make comparisons to the students' decisions as writers.

Mad Talking, Soft Talking, Loud Talking

Good for: when you want students to refine their writing to insert—and hear—their writing voice more assertively

A third exercise, Mad Talking, Soft Talking, Loud Talking, comes from *Inside Out*, a wonderful book by Dan Kirby, Tom Liner, and Ruth Vinz (1988). The purpose of the activity is to "show students inductively that they all use a variety of techniques as part of their writing voices" (143). Voice is one of those intangible parts of writing that all readers know is important, even essential. I think of voice as the measure of confidence the author has in the work. Yet even veteran composition faculty struggle to find ways to describe it, let alone teach it. For instance, when Peter Elbow (1998) considers voice in *Writing with Power*, he readily admits, "Sometimes I fear I will never be clear about what I mean by voice. Certainly I have waxed incoherent on many occasions" (286).

One teacher in my study, Gail Goodwin, used this exercise with her high school creative writing class, composed mostly of seniors. The basic activity, like the others in this chapter, is straightforward, containing only three parts. First, read one of the prompts and give some examples:

- *Mad Talking.* Write a response to a person, thing, or situation that makes you angry.

- *Soft Talking.* Write to comfort a suffering person or thing (an animal, a stuffed animal, even an inanimate object, such as an old car).

- *Fast Talking.* Write to convince someone to do or believe something. Win them over.

Have students think hard about the prompt and then write quickly, for five minutes or so, to capture the emotion they're feeling in their own words. Repeat with each prompt. After the writing is complete, ask students to share and discuss what changed in the writing as the prompts moved from angry to soft to fast. Students should identify specific examples of language usage that might be particular to each speaker. As Kirby, Liner, and Vinz explain, this discussion, which makes an overt connection to technique, is the most important part of the lesson:

> With this exercise, talking about the writings is the key to its success. We call for volunteers to read aloud at least two of their papers, and we talk about how the papers change from one mode to another. We make three columns on the board for Mad Talking, Soft Talking, and Fast Talking, and list under each the stylistic devices used in each kind of writing as they appear in the papers as they are read. (143)

The chart that Kirby and Liner visualize might look something like the chart in Figure 2–10.

On the day that I observed Ms. Goodwin teaching this lesson, a number of students shared their responses to the prompts. One shared a piece about being angry with school cliques, reflecting, "I just grabbed my pen in my angry grip." Another shared his fast-talking piece, which consisted of one sentence, repeated over and over: "Don't kill me; I didn't do it." This occasioned much laughter and good-natured banter. After the sharing, Ms. Goodwin immediately moved on to a new activity about voice, in which she asked students to write in two voices using one of four prompts on the board.

Mad Talking	Soft Talking	Fast Talking
Loaded (strong) language	Rhythmic sentences	Strong verbs
Short sentences	Slow pace	Use of logic
Repetition	Use of conjunctions	Parallel sentence structure

FIG. 2–10 *Characteristics of mad, soft, and fast talking*

Immediately following this, she gave students a homework assignment on dialogue.

Though each activity related to voice, connections were only tacitly made; students had little opportunity to discuss each other's work or to consider what they might learn from the various exercises that they could then apply to future ones. They appeared to enjoy each exercise, and I could see that they were using language in ways well timed for conversation. If Ms. Goodwin were to repeat this activity, then, she might structure it to take advantage of the opportunities that Kirby, Liner, and Vinz intended. For example, students might have gained some insight from reflecting on the contrite language and cautious displacing of blame in Sarah's fast-talking piece, which is addressed to an officer about to write a ticket (see Figure 2–11).

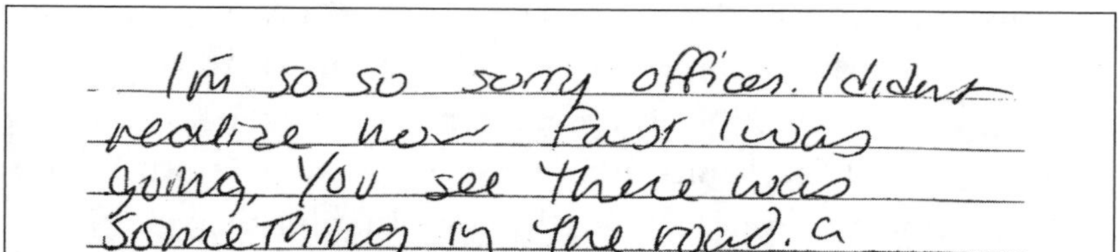

FIG. 2–11 *Sarah's fast-talking piece*

Privately, Ms. Goodwin explained to me that she assigned the Mad, Soft, Fast Talking exercise because it "spurs [students who] are stuck in a certain type of writing rut." She added, "So that's just an exercise, and I didn't expect for them to be like, 'Oh, this is the best thing I've ever written' . . . but I think they had more fun with it than that." Without the reflective conversation, though, her students were unclear about how to interpret or use the activity to learn about writing. Matt, for example, commented that, "I don't think I would use these in writing—mad, soft, and fast talk. . . . I've never read a book where I specifically know that someone's talking fast 'cause it's how I'm reading it." Of the four students I interviewed about the exercise, each listed it lowest of three class activities overall in terms of both interest and "helpfulness to my own writing."

How might we analyze this exercise in light of our three considerations? It has potential for playful engagement, providing students with the free exploration of three different moods through freewriting, a genre intentionally absent of most restrictions, including those of correct mechanics and grammar. Students can have play with emotion and tone, applied to any situation they choose. It offers the opportunity for the teacher to generate a discussion on techniques for capturing emotion and tone, in which students look and listen to what they have created and identify certain characteristics that can be applied to each particular kind of voice. Revisiting the play through the discussion would indeed seem to be the key to the likelihood of students cultivating tone in future writing. Finally, the three-column chart on the board, used to clarify the differences between the three voices, can provide helpful scaffolding. It anchors an abstract discussion of language that develops out of students' own texts, centered on the board for all to see and refer back to later if they wish. It might even prove helpful in responding to literature, as writers analyze fiction by published writers and look at the mechanics behind the mystery of tone and voice.

Steps for the Mad, Soft, Fast Talking Exercise

1. Direct students to freewrite (five minutes each) on the three prompts listed previously.

2. Share in small groups and then have several volunteers read aloud to the whole class as models of each voice.

3. Use the models read aloud to discuss how the writing differed across the three prompts. Ask students to give specific examples to describe the kind of language used in each.

4. As the discussion continues, write students' ideas on the board under the appropriate kind of talking.

5. Possible extensions:
   - Write a story in which one of the characters' voice is mad, soft, or fast.
   - Write a complete piece with a mad, soft, or fast tone.
   - Use what you've learned to identify the tone of one or more short stories and the technique the writer used to achieve that tone.

Further Journeys

There are many more exercises we could look at. A personal favorite, for example, is John Gardner's (1984) prompt to describe a man walking up to his barn after his son's death—without using the words *barn, death,* or *son.* The exercise forces the writer to show us the character's state of mind through his dialogue and behaviors. Other professional writers and composition faculty have produced wonderful exercises that can easily be adapted to the secondary classroom—Wendy Bishop, Ursula LeGuin, Natalie Goldberg, and Anne Lamott, among others. (See Figure 2–12 for some titles.)

Given the three considerations we've explored here, and your own knowledge of your students' interests and needs, the door is open to possibility.

Bird by Bird (Anne Lamott)

Creating the Story: Guides for Writers (Rebecca Rule & Susan Wheeler)

Experiment with Fiction (The Reading/Writing Teacher's Companion) Donald Graves

What a Writer Needs (Ralph Fletcher)

Now Write! Fiction Writing Exercises from Today's Best Writers and Teachers (Sherry Ellis)

Released into Language: Options for Teaching Creative Language (Wendy Bishop)

Steering the Craft (Ursula K. LeGuin)

Working Words: The Process of Creative Writing (Wendy Bishop)

Writing Down the Bones: Freeing the Writer Within (Natalie Goldberg)

(for students) *A Writer's Notebook: Unlocking the Writer Within You* (Ralph Fletcher)

(for poetry) *Awakening the Heart: Exploring Poetry in Elementary and Middle School* (Georgia Heard)

FIG. 2–12 *Books with additional creative writing exercises*

Thus far we have explored how to use play as a jumping off point for writing exercises, balancing it with technique, and steadying the player with scaffolding. Yet taking the writer from these tentative explorations of language to a revised piece of fiction is another matter entirely. We will explore this in Chapter 3, looking particularly at revision strategies and how they can help writers manage the play of fiction.

Managing Play Through Revision

3

The writer is—and should be—drawn in two directions at once and so is the text. In that tension is creativity.

—Donald Murray

Somehow, we must teach our students to distance themselves from what they have written, to get them to see it again, then revise.

—Lester Faigley and Stephen Witte

Writing teachers know the rewards and challenges of engaging students in substantive revision—quite possibly the most fruitful yet difficult phase of the writing process. As Faigley and Witte (1981) observe, the difficulty comes, in part, from the writers' immersion and investment in their original, written text. The teacher's goal, consequently, is to help student writers gain some perspective, increasing the distance between themselves and their drafts. Cognitively, this process is tremendously taxing on writers. Identifying flaws and errors in our own text is more challenging to the working memory than finding the flaws and errors in someone else's text. Why? Because the mind has to differentiate between the writer's *actual intent* (the mental image of the text) and *the physical text* in front of the writer (Vanderberg and Swanson 2007). Specifically, "Students have two texts that must be separated during the revision process: the text they created in their minds and the text they wrote" (749–50).

Another way to think about revision is to consider the delicate balance we've been exploring between play and structure. Words create connections to other words. Ideas flow. Each new written word carries with it connotations, echoes of usage by others. Words are not conjured out of thin air; rather, as literary theorist Bakhtin theorized, the writer "builds on what has gone before by revoicing what has been heard or read, or by exemplifying, adding to, or qualifying what has already been said or written" (Haneda and Wells 2000, 433). As play grows, therefore, words multiply meanings. Linguistic play pulls us here and there, creating its own coherence that may or may not be what we set out to accomplish. For the writer, this play forces a tension between our requirements for the text and our recognition that it can be tremendously difficult to *force the language to say exactly what we want*. Indeed, the writer would be foolish to short-circuit the play by attempting to constrain it too much, for fear of losing generative possibilities and leaps of association. In these cases *the language shows us* what we want, and we often say, "Aha! I hadn't realized that before." Such clarity in learning more about ourselves and our subject is one of the main benefits of revision. As Tom Newkirk (1997) elegantly puts it, the writer uses writing to construct an understanding of self, one "open to the transformative moments that can occur" (14).

Writers experienced with revision seek it out for precisely this reason. Raymond Carver, for example, explains that, "Nearly everything I write goes through many revisions, and I do a lot of backing up, to-and-froing. I don't mind revising; I actually enjoy it, in fact" (McCaffrey and Gregory 1987, 73). But for less experienced writers, the tensions we've just discussed make revision a shaky proposition. Changing one sentence in revision suddenly requires dozens of other reconsiderations, for the writer has broken the chain of meanings that previously helped the ideas to cohere. So much easier, then, to avoid such changes! The flummoxed writer focuses instead on localized edits—fixing words, adding synonyms, and making minor additions or deletions. This pattern is typical for inexperienced writers (Bereiter and Scardamalia 1987; Dix 2006; Emig 1971; Faigley and Witte 1981; Fitzgerald 1987; Perl 1979; Sommers 1980; Yagelski 1995).

And certainly there is a balance to maintain between play and revision. We don't want to kill students' emerging interest in fiction writing by forcing extensive revision onto them. Hardly anyone revises everything they write. And for writers just starting out, it is preferable for them to write as often and as much as possible, gaining fluency in the genre. On the other hand, we do want to offer writers the chance to become more experienced, more technically knowledgeable, and more aware of their own knowledge, by engaging in the revision process. In this chapter I look at metacognitive techniques as well as more hands-on approaches as ways to help novices learn to experience, and potentially enjoy, the power of revision to balance—and even manage—play.

First, a clarification of terms. Some revisions, like celebratory partygoers, make themselves publicly known—they are highly visible to writers and their teachers, showing up via arrows and other marks signifying deletions, additions, substitutions, or various rearrangements of text. I call these *external revisions* because they can be seen on a draft that is edited. In writing instruction, they are usually attended to after a draft has been completed, as part of a formal revision step prior to a second draft. Other, more reclusive, revisions are internally processed. They mysteriously slip into or out of the party with little fanfare within or between drafts. This more internalized form might be characterized by in-the-moment decisions the writer makes within a paragraph or page of text while drafting. A partial sentence deleted in process and retyped differently does not appear on a printed draft—but this *internal revision* is, in its way, influential in changing the text. (The sentence you just read went through four internal revisions before it took its present form on the page.) We'll work with both sorts of revision in this chapter, because both types have a powerful influence on creating effective writing. In both cases, flexible revision strategies help writers manage and shape play by considering issues of structure and form in writing as well as more local issues such as word choice and syntax.

Compass Point, Please: Purpose and Direction

Even after multiple drafts of this chapter, I still find myself grappling with language play—words that head off in the wrong direction and must be regretfully corralled back, and others that help me see a new vista point where I find myself lingering to enjoy the view. So, as a revision strategy of my own, I've decided to take a moment here to focus on purpose and direction. Purpose may be clear by this point—we'll pay attention to ways to manage linguistic and creative play through both internal and external revision strategies.

As for direction—rather than identifying effective *teaching* strategies, I'd like instead to profile effective *writing* strategies that students have taught me, then build upward from there to consider teaching implications. I take this compass point not because of a lack of teaching strategies—on the contrary, classroom teachers provided numerous strategies for students—but, rather, because often the officially sanctioned strategies (such as outlines and character maps) turned out to be troublesome to students; these tools subverted their individual techniques and homogenized the writing process. By focusing on examples of student strategies, I seek to make an argument for the use of metacognitive discussion in the creative writing classroom, to advocate for providing students the opportunity to reflect and learn from their progress and from their peers.

Harnessing Student-Generated Strategies Through Metacognition

If finding the equilibrium discussed in Chapter 1—play balanced with structure, or technique—is difficult for the writer, it may be even more so for the teacher. Historically, teachers have had two choices in teaching writing. As Perl (1979) articulates, the first is to teach the rules of the language, embodied in English grammar, so that students achieve correctness in their writing, enabling them to expand upon their ideas in a legible manner. This practice is troublesome because teaching out of context enables learning out of context—in other words, students do fine on their worksheets, but they leave it all behind as they move on to their own writing, scattering errors right and left. Additionally, this practice may create "a further complication, namely that students begin to conceive of writing as a 'cosmetic' process where concern for correct form supersedes development of ideas" (29). The weight given to correctness disturbs the balance necessary for play; "the excitement of composing, of constructing and discovering meaning, is cut off almost before it has begun" (38).

A second choice, or variation, that teachers have had in teaching writing is to assume that writers know nothing—to label them beginners—and to teach them, collectively, the same ways of approaching the writing task. In this variation, everyone is provided with the same prompt and graphic organizer for outlining or otherwise organizing the information and perhaps even a set of topic sentence starters for each paragraph. Although this approach has the virtue of establishing that each student has been provided with similar support, it also ignores the processes the students carry with them.

My approach to researching and teaching writing builds on Perl's notion that students come into the classroom with established, if unarticulated, strategies for writing, and that unearthing these strategies and reflecting on them in discussion will help students use them more effectively and deliberately. Linda Rief (2007) finds this reflective work so important that she asserts, "Understanding the process in which students engage in order to craft a piece of writing is as important as the final product" (193). In that spirit, I have seeded this chapter with a variety of efficient writing strategies that have been independently developed by students. Although these strategies were not formally recognized in these students' classrooms, they provide a window into the rich possibilities that such articulation offers when writers begin to think about balancing play with craft.

Structuring Strategy: The Working Title

Getting middle and high school students to talk about an abstract concept such as linguistic play isn't easy. I found that it was much easier for them to reflect on the language or behaviors of students in their class than to tackle language play directly. Consequently, whenever I saw opportunities, I recorded students talking with peers about their writing. Often, these discussions evolved into conversations that illustrated certain principles of play. Here is one such transcript.

Suzanne:	Do you guys do titles before or after?
Joanna:	I do it after.
Ceal:	Me too.
Suzanne:	I can never do my title . . . because it takes me too long to start something. I don't know what I'm in the mood for, so I'll . . . title something and then I'll start writing and writing. And all of a sudden the title has . . .
Students together:	Nothing to do with it.
Ceal:	Or I try too hard to make it have sense with the title, and that's not what I want.

When I presented this excerpt in our interview discussions, it quickly resonated with the students. They identified immediately with the titling paradox. By way of explanation, they then shared their related strategies. Several, like Roxanne, described a reluctance to force a work to conform to some preset idea: "If you give it a title at the beginning then you have to write about that title. But if you do it at the end, you can make the title fit to the story more."

Mitch went further than the others, articulating a strategy that balanced language play with organizational focus. He had taken journalism classes for several years and was editor on the school newspaper. In the course of these experiences, he had developed a strategy for managing idea production: a working title that was expected to change by the time the story was finished. When I asked him to identify the connection between the first title and the final piece, he explained, "The first title is what I *intend* to write about. And the changed title is something that relates to what I *actually* wrote about." Mitch subsequently reflected on how this process provided him with some direction, yet allowed for spontaneous thinking:

I start with an idea, and then the idea somehow changes halfway through, or in the beginning. I start writing about something and then I write a sentence that has nothing to do with it, and then all of a sudden, "Oh, that's interesting," and then I play with that aspect of the story. And then usually I like that more, and then I just continue writing about that, and then I have to change it a little bit. So the title doesn't always fit. But I like having a title at the beginning just to know I can kind of relate it to something without having a completely blank screen.

What's useful in Mitch's reflection for the writing teacher? First, it's helpful to have an articulation of an actual writing process from an advanced student writer. Mitch's articulated process differs from the official writing process detailed in posters on the walls of many English classrooms: Prewrite, Organize, Draft, Revise, Edit, Publish. Where in these six steps are students advised that the draft is likely to differ significantly from the prewrite? Or that part of their organizing process might well include anticipating language play? Rather, a neat, linear progression is assumed, except for perhaps repeating the "draft, revise, edit" steps. Yet foundational studies of the writing process have revealed that in addition to the task, the audience, and the writer's prior knowledge, the emerging text itself poses challenges, or constraints, for the writer.

Flower and Hayes (1981) note that, "Just as a title constrains the content of a paper and a topic sentence shapes the options of a paragraph, each word in the growing text determines and limits the choices of what can come next" (371). Mitch's anticipation of two titles helps limit the amount of constraint that the first title has on the piece, allowing him room for play. However, it sets a direction up front, helping him to set goals for his thinking. Mitch's anticipation of a second title helps him think globally, because it helps him maintain constant awareness of the text's direction. This strategy mimics what advanced writers do when they stop at some point in the writing to make "more global decisions, such as 'what do I want to cover here?'" (Flower and Hayes 1981, 371). The in-the-moment changes that Mitch makes as he writes are not cause for alarm, because they will be reflected by a new title once they bring the piece to fruition.

Another reason this reflection is useful for teachers is because it shows the benefit of providing students with an artifact to stimulate reflection and discovery. Such artifacts needn't be very elaborate; they might include a piece of student work, examples of multiple drafts of a title, an introduction, a conclusion, some dialogue picked up by overhearing small groups talk, or some lines jotted down after a pivotal conversation with a friend or colleague. One of my favorite exercises, after students have been working on revising a piece, builds on Peter Elbow's (1973) notion of the *believing and doubting game* that every writer plays. I pose it this way:

> I want you to take a few minutes to think about the two voices you heard in your head while you were working on your writing. Probably one voice is a believing voice. What did that voice say to you? The other voice may be more doubting, arguing, or perhaps it's an adventurous voice, wanting you to write more or write something different. Write this like a play, with Voice 1 and Voice 2 talking to each other. (You might have a Voice 3 spring up too.) See if you can use these voices to capture the internal conversations you engaged in as you wrote.

After presenting the artifact aloud—whether it is students reading their dialogues, performing them with a partner, or just following along on the projector as the teacher reads an excerpt or a brief transcript like the titling one above—it's time for the discussions to happen. Ask students to respond to the artifact: connect, agree, disagree, give an example. If they are silent, give them a few minutes to share in pairs first, or write a response in their journals. Their responses open the door to discussions of linguistic play—something that all writers encounter yet few articulate. In the resulting conversation, teachers can ask students to elaborate, to share their strategies for handling these situations. It may be wise to begin with some of the stronger writers in the class, who can serve as models.

Next, teachers can use this information as a tool to open up those six static steps to the process that students have internalized since elementary school, adding complexity and reflexivity. Students can meet in groups to discuss their own process and create a visual that represents it. They can put that visual on posters and post those on the wall—material for further reflection as the semester, and writing, continues. These ongoing discussions are significant for students because they help writers fill in the gaps between the officially sanctioned writing process and the personal one—the one they know intimately because they struggle with it on a daily basis.

In a Nutshell: Generating Reflection on the Writing Process

- Provide students with an artifact on writing (see the previous section for a list of possibilities, or use the earlier titling conversation). Ask students to write a journal response or warm-up in response: connecting, agreeing, disagreeing, offering an example.

- Generate discussion, using the board or on an overhead to jot down notes on what is said. Wherever possible, ask students to enlarge on their comments: "What do you mean? Tell us more about that. Can you give us an example of how that works in your writing?"

- Ask students to write down what their own writing process is like. Can they jot down the steps they used on their last paper? Or, can they draw it—in cartoon form, as a storyboard? Images can be very revealing: When Holmes and Moulton (1994) asked English language learners to storyboard their writing process, they found that most of the students "demonstrated no prewriting strategies at all" (630). This provides a teacher with great insight into their students' individual understandings of process—and timely opportunities for incorporating supports into the next assignment.

- Group students and ask them to compare their processes. If this is an early discussion, you might ask groups to share what they discovered, and then come to a stopping point. Return to these kinds of conversations again after the next writing assignment.

- When you feel that students have some strategies for planning, composing, and revising, invite them to produce posters illustrating their process. Perhaps there is a metaphor they could sketch and label—is their process like a bike ride? A growing tree? The seasons?

- Ask them to share their posters. In doing so, ask the group to talk about trouble spots in their processes—where they get stuck—as well as strategies—how they get unstuck. Trouble spots can be listed personally or as a class as goals to return to during subsequent lessons and revisions. And if you have room in your classroom, put the posters up as constant reminders of processes in process.

Developing an Organizing Principle: Note Taking

I asked focal students from each of the writing classes in my study to participate in similar kinds of reflective conversations. Matt, who thought of himself as someone who hasn't always "been the best writer or a very good writer," provided insight into another process strategy. Matt worked very hard to compensate for what he saw as a deficit, explaining that he spent extra time on his writing and didn't "just put things together the night before." Matt put a great deal of preparation time into his most challenging assignment, a mystery story. He even read through the class writing textbook, *Writers INC.* (Sebranek, Kemper, and Meyer 2006) in hopes of finding an outline for what a mystery should include, without success. He developed a heightened sense of apprehension about the assignment, later reflecting that he had "absolutely dreaded starting it."

Given this anxiety, it's not surprising that Matt was searching for control over the text before he even started, beginning with that search for an outline. Yet during the actual writing, he found that "it didn't go so bad—you kind of get into it after a while." He developed a routine of writing two pages per day, explaining that he "just started typing it slow, what came out." Still, even with this controlled pacing, the language play kicked in as Matt found himself tangled up in a number of interrelated characters as well as a complicated plot that had yet to unravel completely. He needed an in-the-moment revision technique that would enable him to move the story forward and help him know what new threads to keep (and what to do with them) and which to cut. He found a technique that helped him track the developing information:

I didn't so much go down and create like a formal outline, but when I actually started writing it I started getting confused myself about who the characters were and which person did [the murder] and which person didn't. So I just kind of—as I was writing I would write down like the pool man, and everything I knew about him, like when he was working—I added that in there—and I added that the pool man was Mrs. Casadine's son, what he was doing and what he did that night and everything. I did that for each of the people.

Matt's note-taking strategy (Figure 3–1) helped him keep a handle on his developing ideas without stopping the forward momentum of the story. His choice of words later in our conversation underscored the undetermined, evolving nature of the process: "It eventually *wound up* that the characters were that detective, Mrs. Casadine, the pool man, and the mechanic . . . and I *threw in there* that the pool

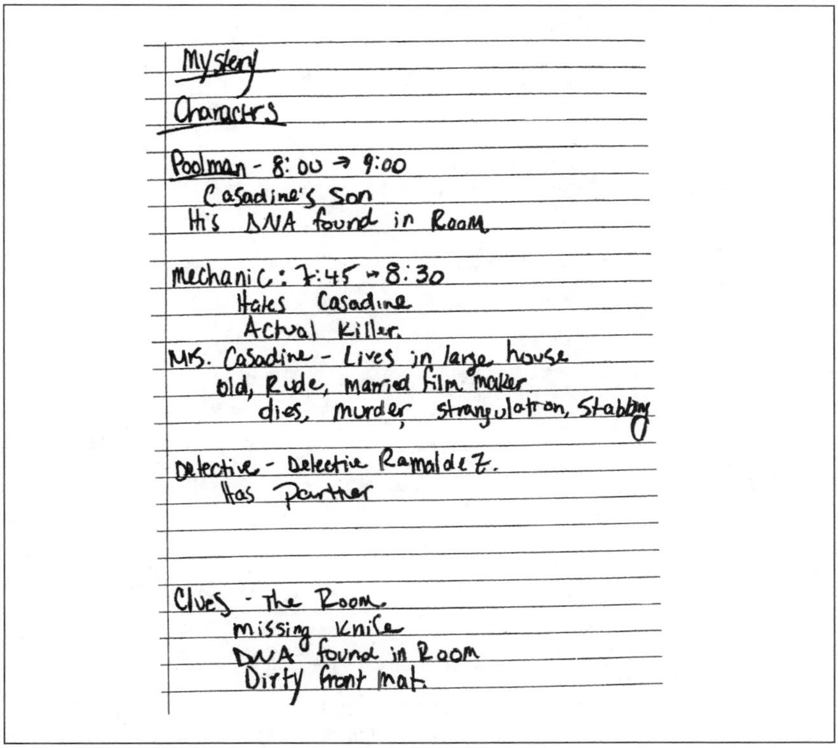

FIG. 3–1 *Matt's notes*

man was actually Mrs. Casadine's son so *maybe* there was a connection there." His completed story benefits from his note-taking strategy, which freed him to focus on developing dialogue and character, as in the excerpt shown in Figure 3–2.

Professional authors often adopt a strategy similar to Matt's, filling notebooks full of information about the characters early in their writing to use as a reference later on. Other writers use talk as a strategy to help clarify characters and plot, dialoging about the book with friends, colleagues, and/or editors. Michael Korda, a former Simon and Schuster editor-in-chief, reminisced about meetings with Jacqueline Susann in which she would "argue points of character motivation and plot, sometimes acting out the parts herself" (Arana 2003, 191). Toni Morrison explained how she would send chunks of her novel *Paradise* to one of her editors, Erroll McDonald, in return for "long,

```
        "Hello Max.  Detective Ramaldes, mind if I ask you a few
more questions?"

        "Go for it."

        "We were just wondering how you inherited 5 million dollars
Josh?"

        "What the hell!  You can't go into my bank accounts!  How'd
you know my real name was Josh?"

        "Actually, with probable cause, we can, and we did.  We
already got your little friend.  He's already been taken down
town for further questioning and a proper lock up.  Why don't
you just make it easier on us, and you, and just tell me what
happened."

        "Honestly, It wasn't me.  I'll tell you the whole story.  I
didn't do anything.  As you now know, I am Mrs. Casadine's son.
She had just come in for the night at around 8:00 or so.  Jason
was finishing working on the computer upstairs.  He was done by
about 8:15.  I told him that I would be a little while longer,
```

FIG. 3–2 *An excerpt from Matt's first full-length story*

interesting letters" that "contain information about what's strong, what's successful, what troubles him, what stands out as being really awful, that kind of thing. Which is what you want" (Jaffrey 2000). These strategies take place during drafting; they represent moments when these authors pause in the writing to figure something out, to gain some understanding from the emerging text—and make some critical decisions. They're not neat, well-organized points on an outline but tend to include messy scribbling on ripped pieces of paper or a notebook page damp from the hand of a writer who has just figured something out, in the shower.

Student writers need the opportunity to pause during composing to clarify and expand their thinking, too. When teachers help students learn revision strategies, they give these novice writers a better chance of navigating the play/structure balance. As students learn to play like writers, teachers can encourage them to use their journals to figure out story ideas in the moment.

As we might expect, Matt's notebook strategy was successful in helping him complete his first full-length story. By the end of the semester, his teacher commented specifically on his sense of focus and voice, adding, "He's just able to handle more diversity than I saw in the beginning."

Matt himself expressed a tremendous sense of accomplishment at having completed such a long and daunting task: "It was kind of self-satisfying when you were done with it, just looking back at it," he explained. "I have written twelve-page papers before, but those are like research papers and all that kind of stuff, but I've never really written a *story*."

Matt's strategy also sheds light on process problems for teachers of writing. For the most part, the students I worked with—both inexperienced and more advanced student writers at the middle and high school level—had little trouble beginning their fiction. They took hold of an idea or a character or a task (such as those suggested in Chapter 2) and once that first paragraph was down, they moved ahead easily enough. As Raymond Carver puts it, the writing of the first line "shoves" the writer onto the second, and then "the process begins to take on momentum and acquire a direction" (McCaffrey and Gregory 1987, 73). Matt's experience with his mystery story and his struggle to keep track of characters as the plot changed and grew showcases problems that crop up midway through the writing, when the momentum really takes off. Or, as Matt's classmate John explained in an interview:

> I was working on [my mystery story] the other day and I had four or five pages done and I realized . . . it's all very much an introduction to the character before I even got into the story. So I think I'm going to have a problem like Matt, where it's already five or six pages and I barely have any story material.

The challenges that these students expressed surprised me because their teacher, Ms. Goodwin, had given them an assignment to create an extensive character sketch before they started writing. (See Figure 3–3 for a copy of the assignment.) Student accounts indicated, however, that completing this seventeen-item worksheet actually hindered their story development. Sarah pointed out that she had "spent three pages introducing the detective and now I don't know what's happening so I have to figure that out." Matt wondered why they had to complete so much information about the character, noting that it wasn't necessary to know so much, "to the point that you know if the character works out every Thursday."

I felt obligated to point out that perhaps it was background information—material the author needed to know, even if it was not evident in the story itself. Professional writers often do background research and note taking to explore character and plot in advance of writing the story. Patricia Cornwell, for example, writes that without this research, she "could not grasp the characters nor understand what they felt" (Arana 2003, 153). This idea was soundly rejected by these novice writers, who were grappling with enough constraints as it was. Research supports their response, suggesting that what works for professional writers may not be immediately

CREATIVE WRITING

MYSTERY...

CHARACTER SKETCH

This sketch should be about 1-2 characters from your mystery, preferably the detective(s), and include the following (remember the more bizarre the idiosyncracies the better):
Name
Date of Birth
Dress
Physical Description
Physique and Looks
Marital Status
Personal Habits
Mannerisms and Idiosyncracies
Recreation
Home
Office and "help"
Car
Weapons
M.O.
Code of Ethics
Fees
Additional Background (i.e. family, place/country of birth, what led them into the private detective field, "baggage" etc.)

THE MYSTERY

Your mystery must contain the following elements to be successful:
- A well-developed (see above) detective/main character.
- Descriptive, fresh, and original setting.
- A Motive (if a Murder Mystery).
- At least one, (preferably more) Red Herrings to throw the reader and perhaps the detective off the trail.
- Descriptive, original story that makes sense and is believable.
- Interesting language and either dialogues or monologues where we get into the head of the detective and possibly other characters.

This assignment should be no less than 10 pages typed at completion. In order to effectively develop the story and your main character, and not fall into a "cliche storyline" trap, it is necessary to have some length to it. Mysteries are inherently bizarre, deceptive, multifaceted, and can have limitless twists and turns. Have *fun* with it!

FIG. 3–3 *A character sketch form that actually hindered writing*

useful to novices. Indeed, it's likely that giving developing writers too much information to hold in working memory forces them to discard information in order to develop more essential story elements (Bereiter and Scardamalia 1987).

Making the Fiction Worksheet
Productive: Flexibility and Timing

The lesson I took away from these students in regard to using creative writing preparation worksheets in the classroom was twofold. First, when supplying formal strategies for managing play, make them flexible—malleable enough for students to allow the story to develop in multiple directions and to use their own processes to work within them. Damien, an advanced writer, developed a stunningly effective—and unusual—strategy: He simply cut the list of questions on the character sketch worksheet in half and included only ones that were essential to his story or that he was prepared to answer at that point in the process. (Figure 3–4 shows one of his character sketches.)

Name: Reginald Denny

Age: Early 40's

Occupation: Taxi cab driver

Marital Status/ Family background: Divorce due to a drinking problem. The divorce, however, eventually convinced him to seek help. Reginald has very little family to speak of except for an uncle who owns a bar.

Hobby: When there is little else to do Reginald will play with his Zippo cigarette lighter he found once while he was a teenager.

Demeanor: Reginald is a quiet man because he very rarely has anything important to say or anyone to share it with.

Friends: They call him Reggie and that's all we know about them.

Personality: All his life people have looked at Reggie and he never liked it. During his days of alcohol abuse, wandering eyes never bothered him. Now, however, since he has stopped drinking he finds that people are looking at his more and more everyday. Thank god there is still the good old Zippo lighter.

FIG. 3–4 *Damien's customized list of character traits*

By customizing the worksheet, Damien prevented an overload of information at the beginning of the process, yet he planned far enough to guide the story in productive directions—giving his fictional play some focus and direction and reducing the amount of revision required later. Would most students feel free to complete only half of the assignment? Not likely. Yet if the assignment had asked them to select only a handful from a larger list of characteristics to develop their character, it would have gone a long way toward reducing constraints. Add in time for students to share with one another, and we've incorporated dialogue that enables writers to anticipate reader reactions early in the writing process.

The second lesson I learned from working with Matt and his peers relates to timing. Despite the difficulty that writers expressed in the *midst* of composing, most graphic organizers or character/story sketches—and every one that I saw used in classrooms—are targeted to the prewriting process, prior to drafting. Yet it is *during* drafting, with its internal, in-the-moment revisions, and later, during external revision, when students appear to need the most help. As psychologists Vanderberg and Swanson (2007) explain, producing the actual text is especially difficult because it uses all of the components of the writing process at once: "Writers will sometimes edit and plan during text production, and they will sometimes plan and produce new text during revision" (749). Or, let's consider a students' perspective, which Janice offers: "I find that getting started isn't that hard. It's actually the dialogue and keeping it interesting that makes it hard for me."

So why focus all of the students' energies on planning prior to writing? In another creative writing class I studied, the teacher's prewriting assignment asked students nine questions, ranging from a description of the characters they planned to use, to a list of both major and minor complications, to an explanation of the climax of the as-yet-unwritten story. (See Figure 3–5 for a copy of this assignment.) These are questions that all fiction writers consider at some point. But be careful of too much planning in advance, which can actually stifle play.

```
                    CREATE  A SHORT STORY FROM
                    A REAL LIFE SITUATION

       1.  Most writers of articles are told to keep in mind the four w's and one h.
   (who, what, when, where, and now)  Usually they are asked to have all this vital infor-
   mation in the first paragraph of the article.  Using the article you have chosen to use,
   list these basic elements first.

   2. List the questions you have asked about the article.

   3. List the characters you plan to use in your short story and give a brief description.

   4. List and briefly describe the c̶h̶a̶r̶a̶c̶t̶e̶r̶s̶  setting(s) which will appear in your story.
      (time and place)

   5. List what will be your main conflict (ie. man versus man) and tell specifically who
      will be involved.  (John Doe vs John Q Public)

   6. List any minor conflicts and explain briefly as in #5.

   7. List and briefly describe the major complication.  (Harry Kellerman is under too
      much pressure from too many sources.)

   8. List and briefly explain any minor complications.  (Paula cannot control the children,
      Paula's bridge group stays too latem etc.)

   9. Briefly explain the climax.  (resolution of conflict)  ((Kellerman commits suicide))

   10. Begin to write your story keeping the following in mind:
         a/ alternate showing and telling to increase interest
         b/ remember that there are four ways an author may develop a character, try to
            do more than simply describe and tell about the character; get inside his head,
            tell what he is ·thinking; use dialog, both form the main character and any
            minor characters; use actions

   11. Because a short story is short, the writer is limited in space; therefore, straight
      character or setting description must be limited.

   12. The opening action (usually the first paragraph or so) usually tells the main setting,
      usually introduces the main character, and may hint at or actually set forth the mian
      conflict.

   13. The rising action (the bulk of the story) develops the conflict throught̶/̶d̶h̶/̶  the
      complications.  The minor characters and their relationship to the main character
      is revealed.

   14. The climax will be the resolution of the major (and possibly minor) complication
      or conflict.

   15. The falling action or the denouement will be the tying up of any loose ends, often
      minor complications.
```

FIG. 3–5 *Prewriting form that stifled play*

This particular assignment stimulated resistance among the students. One argued, "I don't understand why I have to fill out these questions—I probably won't use any of it. I'll probably change all of it except the name." The teacher walked from desk to desk, saying, "It's just a starting point." Given the power of language play, chances are that she was right about the limited staying power for these ideas. She knew the pull of language play and indicated to me that she intended the worksheet only to get students started—expecting that they would change as they wrote. For students with little fiction-writing experience, however, the task of planning the whole scope of a story before they had begun created tension, stimulated apprehension, and restricted possibilities for playful exploration. As a result, students that I interviewed largely ignored the planning sheet once it was completed. However, this activity could be quite useful if it were pared down to essentials—the characters, their initial conflict, and a setting—prior to writing and *offered again midway through the process* or at the end of the first draft as a way to take stock of the developing story and guide subsequent revisions.

Using a set of questions or guides selectively and asking students to tailor it to their needs throughout the process also resolves another problem that teachers and students alike report with prewriting organizers: Students rarely use them once they start drafting. As Denise graphically illustrated with a piece of paper meant to represent her prewriting assignment: "I took my piece of paper, the outline, and *zzzzzzzzzzzp!* I just ripped it. I didn't even have it anymore. I ripped it in half and just started writing." When teachers help students apply the organizer to their actual text in the midst of, or after, initial production, they can make the purpose of plotting out key points in a story more clear. The organizer can be used as a tool for writers to resee their story.

Here's an example of how this might work in practice. Maria has answered a few key questions: perhaps two about character, one about setting, and one on conflict. Then she sets out to write an initial text, a first draft. Halfway through, she gets stuck, tangled up in a story that is seemingly heading nowhere and everywhere at the same time. This is a good time for some reseeing. The teacher gives Maria several more questions to answer about her story. The questions particularly relate to unfolding the plot. The teacher gives two other students in the class the same questions and asks them to pair up with Maria. Through talking about her own story as well as her two classmates' stories, Maria realizes what she wants to do with this piece. She jots down a plan, confers with the teacher, and is ready to revise and continue. Maria may need to repeat this process a couple more times before she reaches the end.

What is useful in this admittedly optimistic example? First, in terms of Maria's growing understanding of process, it assumes that text generation and revision are intertwined. Maria is getting the message that revision is part of her practice—an essential part to consider at key stopping points, not just something tacked on at the end. (This is one reason my revision chapter is in the middle of this book, and not the last chapter—we need to think about it throughout the process.) Second, in light of the necessary play/structure balance for successful fiction, it gives Maria a tool to rein in play once it's taken her somewhere; it helps her untangle the storylines and find the coherence at the heart of the story once it is somewhat formed. And finally, in terms of authorial motivation, it gives Maria readers—an audience to write for—and a sounding board for dialogue and feedback. Each of these benefits reduces the cognitive difficulty of the overall task by providing support at a critical junction.

In a Nutshell: Targeting First Draft, In-the-Moment Revision
- One area to consider prior to writing is reading short stories as models in the genre and inspirations for future writing. I like to pull a range of pieces, drawing from published texts in short story anthologies, from writing contests in local newspapers, and from published student writing found in sources such as *Teen Ink*. Using the mixture rather than only drawing on masterpieces in literature makes writing appear more attainable to students. These models can be read prior to, during, or after composing a first draft, to help guide the writer in thinking about what revisions make sense and feel right. We'll explore this further in Chapter 5, which includes questions to aid students in reading these stories from a writer's perspective. Reading primes students to write.

- During prewriting, have students describe at least two characters, a setting, a conflict, and a rough sense of what might happen in the story. Do not use more than six questions, so they will really spend time focusing and thinking and directing their thinking. Ask them to start composing a couple of pages based on these characters.

- After the first couple of pages are drafted, have students exchange papers with one or more readers to get feedback on their in-process piece. Here's a good place to pose a few questions about the progression of events in the story. What happens next? What do your readers expect to find out? What is promised in the story so far? Where is the logical next place for these characters to go? Ask the writers to jot down in more detail the plot as it is unfolding. This will help guide their ongoing writing and internal revision decisions.

- Have students continue to revise their piece, using their notes to help them.

- Ask students to submit the complete draft along with a paragraph or two of reflection on their process: How closely does this piece resemble their planning? What helped them the most along the way? What questions do they still have about their story?

- For students who struggle with spelling and/or vocabulary, provide a word bank on the board, the wall, or individually. Have students add to the word bank as they inquire about new words.

Managing External Revision: Reshaping a Text

In this section we move on to external revision—the kind that leaves marks on the page (preferably, all over the page)—and results in a more focused, streamlined next draft. Student fiction writers need very specific kinds of strategies to help with formal revision—ones that cultivate continuing play, allow for independence and diversity in approaches, and demand both local and global attention. In other words, the strategy needs to help the writer entertain changes both at the word and sentence level *and* identify how those changes may alter the overall plot, character, or thematic development. No small feat.

Perhaps in reaction to the perceived difficulty of teaching this phase of the process, one teacher in my study ignored revision altogether, reflecting, "I sometimes wonder if you spend too much time trying to make one piece perfect—if you kill the interest, the spontaneity, the enjoyment of creative writing. And that's not my goal, I guess." It's a fair point; I'm not advocating killing the play of writing through endless revision and editing. Yet revision can be a pivotal stage, one where play is refined, where the story reaches its full potential and writers can achieve a new understanding about themselves and the world. In revision, meaning is questioned, words challenged, themes realized, and characters reshaped. Sadie, for example, used revision as a sort of paper version of a think-aloud about her text (see Figure 3–6). Her local and global revisions show her deep investment in her work.

Rather than focusing on over-revising and potentially killing the spontaneity and motivation for writing, let's think about how writers play with revision. As we have throughout this chapter, let's explore these ideas through a student's experience—again using a strategy developed independently from instruction—and then look at this experience from a teacher's perspective and see what it tells us in terms of teaching revision.

Kevyn, described by his teacher as "a real thinker," commented at one time that he especially enjoyed our interview sessions because

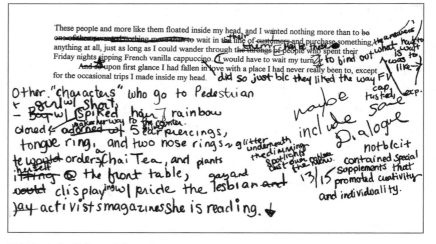

FIG. 3–6 *Sadie's revisions*

they provided him with an opportunity to "talk about my writing like a writer, instead of just as a student." Still, despite being deeply invested in the whole writing experience, wanting to experiment with symbolic and thematic considerations, Kevyn found himself bumping up against language play at its most basic. In one of our interviews, he ruefully admitted, "A lot of times I don't have direction... and I just type it all at once and it just comes out into this one big clump of writing." At times this created real difficulties as he struggled to create coherence from "the clump." In a written analysis of his creative writing journal turned in as an honors project, Kevyn described how one such struggle eventually derailed the first piece he wrote for the class:

> I began writing "The Story on Page One" as a series of notes and observations about my attitudes at the time. These notes seem random, chaotic and out of order and that is because my thoughts at the time were random, chaotic, and out of order. From these notes, I wrote something that resembled an essay. Before I finished the essay, though, I found myself writing about characters, a setting, and other components of a story. . . . Transforming random notes into a story proves to be the most difficult task when writing. I had too much to say and wasn't accurate enough with my language to keep the story interesting. As a result I rambled and I feel that I lost the attention of the reader.

Kevyn subsequently discovered that he could counteract this difficulty, however, through a number of strategies that he used during the revision process. This process is highlighted here with a series of excerpts from a story Kevyn wrote called, "A Ladybug in the Garden," which Kevyn felt "thoroughly demonstrates [his] writing process from start to finish."

Kevyn wrote the original draft of "A Ladybug in the Garden" into his notebook by hand, taking full advantage of linguistic play to actively generate thoughts and make connections to other ideas as they occurred and as relationships became clearer. This is most clearly shown by a profusion of arrows and inserts that signal spontaneous

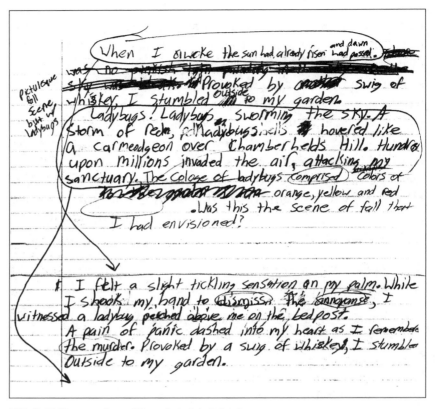

FIG. 3–7 *Excerpt from Kevyn's initial draft*

jumps in thinking (see Figure 3–7). Yet with his writer's eye, Kevyn remained constantly aware of the structural possibilities of these developing texts, and he marked that awareness through marginal comments such as the "picturesque fall scene but w/ladybugs." By flagging global intentions for local text excerpts, he retained control and focus over the developing piece.

Kevyn then took the original story from its "all scattered" state and typed it on the computer, making the changes that were indicated by arrows in the original draft—additions, deletions, substitutions, and rearrangements (see Figure 3–8). He retained the flexibility to make additional changes as they occurred to him. The second sentence, for example, is new, the product of internal revision between the drafts. It connects the narrator intimately to the ladybugs through physical touch—"I felt a slight tickling sensation on my palm"—leading to a sense of panic and a swig of whiskey, the latter phrase moved down in this revision to follow the physical sensation and show its effect. Only then—with the reader now fully aware of the narrator's state of mind—does Kevyn bring the ladybugs in a swarm from the sky. Although he has already made an effective change, he is open to flexibility. Rather than stopping the play and shortcutting the momentum of the story when he needs a word, he types "*p*" *word* to represent a word he cannot remember and plans to look up later. After typing his draft, Kevyn takes another pass through, writing additional revisions by hand, flagging continuing or unresolved issues—such as the question mark over "like a carmeodgeon" [sic].

Kevyn told me he then fine-tuned his work by showing it to his mother and asking others for help, especially in "centering [his] focus . . . on exactly where [he wanted] to go with the piece." Although nobody showed Kevyn how to create this process, his teacher, Matt Phillips, offered a curriculum that heavily supported and encouraged it, for students were required to revise each piece a couple of times

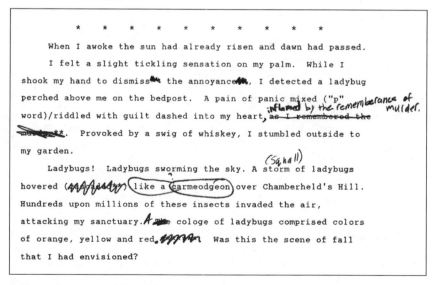

FIG. 3–8 *Kevyn's revised draft*

and to seek written advice from several other readers. (The advantages of this curriculum are explored in Chapter 5.) In this case, Kevyn's mother had filled out a response form, indicating that she liked the description in the piece, was "surprised how the story changed in mood, action, and description once the ladybugs were introduced," and found the piece somewhat Poe-like and clever. Kevyn's teacher concurred with these comments, admiring the story as "gruesome, tortured, maniacal, in a concealed way, hidden behind overly mannered language." The changes in the excerpts shown here suggest that Kevyn deliberately used both phases of his writing process to shape this tone and style, and he did so successfully. At the end of the semester, Kevyn told me that revision allowed him "to actually focus on where I want the writing to go."

What can teachers learn about revision from Kevyn's example that might support a whole class of writers working at different levels—advanced, novice, and reluctant? Let's break down Kevyn's process into its individual components:

- Flagging intentions while writing

- Redrafting in a different medium (typing from handwritten text, etc.)

- Revising the draft by hand

- Getting written feedback from readers

- Commenting verbally and in writing on the revising process

These components suggest three useful class activities: text annotation, selectively required mixed-media revisions, and required use of multiple readers with written feedback forms. Let's look at each phase individually.

Text Annotation

As part of a different study, a school–university collaboration with middle school English teachers called the Partnership for Literacy

(Adler and Rougle 2005), my colleagues and I found that the use of text annotations supported reluctant and inexperienced readers as they worked to make personal meaning from texts. One teacher developed a set of "readers' marks" as she called them, for helping students annotate their class readings. Students wrote symbols in the margins, such as an exclamation point for something in the text that surprised them. Given the interrelatedness of reading and writing practices, it is logical that such annotations would also work for writers rethinking their own writing (and perhaps for the writers' peers who are providing feedback). Some possible marks appear in the chart in Figure 3–9.

Some of the marks target the local level (looking at word choice, inserting description into a sentence) and some target the global level (moving or deleting chunks, rewriting sections). This approach also has the benefit of flexibility. Teachers may advise students to use only the marks that make sense to them or fit the assignment. (Imagine the frustration of hunting around for a word to circle, just to be able to check that off the list!) Students might also develop their own shorthand, as Kevyn did, to better fit their needs.

→ = move this text to another part of the paper

◯ = find another word

^ = needs more description; insert something here

D = Add dialogue here?

? = Not sure if this works. Need to ask someone.

?? = I know this isn't working; it doesn't feel right. Need to freewrite on this section again.

X = Delete this for now.

Consider making up your own marks, too.

FIG. 3–9 *Writers' marks*

Selectively Required Mixed-Media Revisions

Why are mixed-media revisions "selectively" required? Why shouldn't teachers require students to revise each piece? Because in addition to the evidence gained through practical experience, research also shows that more is not necessarily better. Having inexperienced writers revise does not necessarily produce better writing (Perl 1979). And few experienced writers revise every piece—it would be a good way to learn to hate writing, to undo the benefits of play. So select pieces that are meaningful for students, or better yet, let them select their own pieces for revision—and help them revise those pieces all the way. Students in one class I studied wrote a great deal each month, but they were only required to choose two substantive creative pieces for full-fledged revision each quarter. (This limitation also helped the teacher handle the paper load that inevitably results from lots of writing.) This approach encouraged student writers to take intellectual risks and also helped ensure that when they did revise, they were motivated to do so, because they had deliberately chosen a piece that mattered to them.

Why mixed media? By observing students writing in classes I've taught as well as in the ones I've studied as a researcher, I've found that those who write and revise directly on the computer—or entirely by hand—are prone to making only surface-level changes. Researchers comparing revisions done on word processors to those made with pen and paper report similar results (Daiute 1986).

Some time ago I decided to model my own revision practices for my college students in an upper-division writing class. I projected a document showing revisions made visible by the Track Changes feature in Microsoft Word. All of a sudden the relaxed mood changed. People sat forward, intently curious. Someone asked, "What is that stuff on the right-hand side?" I realized that this could be a tool for students. After showing them how to use the tracking feature, I sent them home to do revisions, suggesting that some might use it to keep track of deletions as well as comments and additions to the text. What surprised me when students came back the following week was not that only a few students had actually tried using the tool—that was to be expected—but that the few who had tried it—all inexperienced writers—spoke about it as a transformative experience. I asked them what was so great about revising with the changes tracked as opposed to their typical computer-based revising. "It saves what you delete," they said unanimously. Somehow this made it safe to cut text.

That was an aha moment for me as a writing teacher. Of course reluctant writers are not going to cut text. No wonder they do not delete at the global level or move chunks around. Just getting the first chunk down is an achievement in itself. Who wants to risk tampering with that precious page of text filling the screen, helping to meet the project's page-length requirements? Yet when they used the tracking feature, they knew they could always select the "reject changes" option and all would be as before. It gave them permission to play.

In a way, printing out typed text and making handwritten changes on it, as Kevyn did, has the same effect—it does not irrevocably alter the original text. The tried-and-true method of using scissors and tape to cut and paste revisions on a copy of the original text works as well, for the same reason. Yet students are, for some reason, largely reluctant to try that. Perhaps it seems juvenile to them, or wasteful of time, or silly. Whatever approach students take to revision, ask them to try using mixed-media: writing in pencil on printed text, typing up handwritten text, placing sticky notes on either handwritten or typed text, tracking changes on electronic text, or cutting and pasting a copy of the printed text.

Any of these approaches will elicit more global revisions and provide students with the flexibility to alter the constructed words without penalty; they can always return to the original manuscript if they wish. In terms of equilibrium, the existing text provides students with the grounding, a set of boundaries guiding their next steps; the mixed-media approach offers them the opportunity to play with that text—without risk. It challenges the permanent power of the printed word and opens the physical text up to insertions and deletions, while leaving the new text in dialogue with the existing one, *with the dialogue made visible* by the mixed media.

Required Use of Multiple Readers with Written Feedback

When I ask students if they like to receive peer feedback, I get a mixed response. Those who don't like it complain about readers who "tell you nothing about your story except 'it's good, don't change a thing'"; readers who are overly critical; readers who mark all over the text correcting errors but say nothing substantial about the story itself. But these same students admit that when peer feedback works, it's a wonderful thing. In the high school study, for example, Kurt came to rely on feedback for a sense of how well his work was playing to his audience. (More on this in Chapter 4.)

So setting some clear ground rules is useful when introducing peer feedback to a class. Figure 3–10 contains a list of Dos and Don'ts that I review with students before they enter into formal peer feedback groups. In my classes, students meet in groups of two to four to share their stories and get feedback. They often meet again with the same group a bit later on to show revisions to the piece, maintaining a sense of continuity. I cannot recall where I heard the line "Do not try to decide whether the writer is going to heaven or hell," but it gets a chuckle from students, and they take its point to heart.

After students meet in peer feedback groups, I save ten minutes for quiet written reflection in a writing journal. I ask students to respond to three questions on the board: What did you hear during your conference today? What are your goals for your writing in light of this feedback? How will you tackle these goals? This reflective writing helps students cement the learning they've gained from their peers so they will remember it once they get home, or in the future in class. It also gives them a strategy for shaping the play that will come as they continue writing.

Another teacher whom I observed handled peer feedback a little differently. Mr. Phillips prepared feedback forms for students, providing just a couple of open-ended questions to encourage lengthy responses. (See Figure 3–11 for an example.) Students could exchange their paper and form with anyone in or outside of class and get written feedback. They then attached that feedback to their final draft when they handed it in. Peer feedback gives students an audience to write for, suggestions for revision, and the motivation to

	DO	**DO NOT**
Writers	• Share your questions with your group at the beginning. • Direct the discussion by asking your questions. • Take notes on what is said.	• Explain what you were trying to do. (*Listen to what you did do. Then write some notes about what you still need to do.*) • Take offense. Questions really do help.
Readers	• Mark with a wavy line anything you especially like. • Put a question mark by what you don't understand. • Think about the writer's questions; make margin notes. • Tell the author what you experienced as a reader and what made you experience it that way.	• Correct grammar or spelling. (Say there are some errors. Later you can say what they are, time permitting.) • Ask questions about what the author was trying to do. • Be hypercritical, sarcastic, "mean," or "nice"; do be honest, fair, and humane. • Try to decide whether the writer is going to heaven or hell.

FIG. 3–10 *Dos and don'ts in peer feedback groups*

General reactions to the piece:

Wow - this piece has so much feeling in it I am feeling through your words what you are going through.

Really good descriptions - especially the contrasting ones (like what you have in the beginning, and then don't in the end)

Specific thoughts/suggestions for improvement or direction:

Expand the middle part where you talk about the life in NYC - about making the decision and what it means to you

FIG. 3–11 *Mr. Phillips' feedback form*

make substantial changes. In this case, students especially appreciated the opportunity to share their writing with parents and extended family, who surprisingly offered remarkably constructive advice regardless of their relationship to the author.

In a Nutshell: Managing External Revision

- Separate revision (global and local text changes) from editing (corrections for usage).

- Be selective when choosing texts that require formal revision. Select (or ask students to do so) ones that are meaningful and have high motivation.

- Model text annotations for writers to help them learn how to flag their intentions for changes large and small.

- Ask students to revise in a different media than their original text, writing on computer-generated printouts, using sticky notes, cutting and pasting by hand, or trying the Track Changes feature in Microsoft Word.

- Require multiple readers of texts selected for revision. Use peer feedback groups, written feedback forms, or some other variation that you find to be effective.

Chapter 3 is fittingly a midpoint in this book, for we want the focus on revision to be center stage rather than a last step or an afterthought. The strategies explored here may be used as students extend the writing approaches and exercises discussed in Chapter 2 or as support for the unprompted writing approaches that follow next, in Chapter 4. Then, in the final chapter, we'll look for ways to integrate revision throughout the creative writing curriculum.

Unprompted Writing

Learning How Writers Play

We write what we don't know about what we know.
— Grace Paley

Thus far we've explored ways to generate play through writing exercises (Chapter 2) and ways to help writers manage play through both internal and external revision practices (Chapter 3). These are the nuts and bolts of teaching creative writing: Provide writing exercises to get the fiction going and help writers craft it into more polished prose. And if our only goal was to give students instruction in fiction, then we could wrap this up. However, if our goal is to help students become writers, then we need to add a critical piece: how to help students *find their own material and reshape it for a real audience*. This is what writers do.

I'll use myself as an example. When I'm in the writing groove—usually during the summer when I don't have teaching concerns on my plate—I pay attention to my experiences and surroundings in a different way. I *notice*. I jot ideas down on scraps of paper or in my journal. Here is one such experience:

> One summer in Albany, New York, I was going into a bank downtown, one with a swinging door that could both push in and pull out. A man approached with an ambling gait, walking like he had a large wheel attached to one foot that he couldn't quite shake loose. His thick brown hair, streaked with grey and dirt, bunched up in the front and then slid some ways

down his back; his too-large white button-down shirt hung untucked and grease-stained. Sharp blue eyes and a crooked smile belied his condition, accompanied as they were by blistered lips and yellow teeth. He walked too close; he pointed at me; he pushed at my shoulder; his blue eyes plunged a hard, inquisitive look at my reticent hazel ones. He put his left hand on the push bar on the door.

"Push or pull? Push or pull? PUSH OR PULL?" he demanded. It seemed, the more he repeated it, a metaphysical question. "Pull," I said quietly, slipping around him and into the bank. As I looked back, he nodded to himself a few times, saying something under his breath, then darted off, making a quick left at the corner. I stood uneasily in line, wondering whose fate I had decided with that question.

It's an anecdote, more fanciful as time passes. I could tell it at a party or share it with a friend over lunch, both of us shaking our heads and laughing. Or I could write it down on one of those scraps of paper that hold my writing ideas, and save it as potential material. As soon as I pick that scrap of paper up again, I begin thinking of my real experience differently, beyond reflection and entertainment. I see multiple perspectives in that single event. I have to think about it from different angles. I have to think what a narrator would do with that. Who might tell this story? Me? Him? A bank teller? An omniscient narrator who can see into both of our heads?

Once I begin to switch perspectives on the real event, I come to think about myself—as a person—differently. I see my own prejudices against the homeless, my fear of mental illness, my reluctance to engage with the unknown. I see institutions differently—the irony of the man asking the question in front of a bank, a house of money that stores the cash that would get him off the streets. He might well be asking, "Deposit or withdrawal? Deposit or withdrawal?"

I see alternate possibilities for my own actions, as I think about myself as a character with plot potential. What happened earlier that morning? What does the woman do after the man confronts her? What choices does she have? What if he returns? Would she call security? Engage in his conversation? And the reader—with whom would the reader sympathize?

As a writer, I find that the opportunities to explore my own experiences in fiction, and to seek feedback from the readers that help shape my text, offer potential for two kinds of development. First, I earn the ability to develop deeper understandings of my own actions and those around me, by stepping out of my own shoes. I begin to see my actions through the larger scope of fiction, which necessitates flexibility. In changing characters from reality, manipulating them, and expanding upon events, I see characters grow and change. As Ursula LeGuin (1998) puts it, "Even if it's just a trip down a super-market aisle or some thoughts going on inside a head, [a story] should end up in a different place from where it started. That's what narrative does. It goes. It moves. Story is change" (xii). And because it's my story to develop, it's meaningful in a special way, intensifying my attention to feedback, increasing the possibility of revision, and increasing my motivation to sand down and reshape parts of the story.

Murray (1989) described a similar shift that occurred when he wrote a poem based on an incident from his childhood. The retelling changed as he brought a second character into the poem and reconceived the situation. In retrospect, he observed that by changing the telling of the incident, he irrevocably altered the way he now remembers it. As he explained, "The poem that was for a few seconds imaginary has become autobiographical by being written" (70).

As the story progresses, it's likely that the writer will also grow. In writing my bank story, I am likely to learn, at least tacitly, about what drives people to act the way they do—I learn to watch and interpret physical expressions, behaviors, dialogue, nonverbal movement. Feedback from my readers tells me how they see human development—and fiction development—and my learning continues. I grow because taking this real event into an imaginary place helps me explore the possibilities and mysteries in human nature.

That this growth is likely to be subconscious does not diminish its importance; children at play may not realize that they are exploring possibilities for their future decisions and plans, yet they are likely to draw upon those understandings in the future. Vygotsky hypothesized that a change so powerful in one area of thinking has the potential to "influence all the other functions and change the child's conscious relation to the world"—including, among other things, "perception, logical memory, intentional attention, abstract thinking, and scientific imagination" (Hedegaard 2007, 249). The willful reimagining of an everyday event helps the writer learn about fiction; as an added bonus, it offers rich possibility for extending students' thinking in many other ways.

In short, students who learn to play like writers benefit from both the play and the writing—the push and the pull, if you will. Negotiating lived experiences produces more successful fiction and more developed selves. This premise is at the heart of this chapter. We'll look at the writing of students and the work of teachers to learn both about the restrictive effects of prompts and the depth of thought that emerges with permission to play.

Yet as with our earlier explorations of play, tensions emerge. In this case, the twin benefits of fictional play—the *individual's* desire to explore and play with reality and the *writer's* increased desire to craft that reality into effective fiction—collide. While real-world experience forms the foundation for story play, the genre of fiction sets up expectations that contain, shape, and reimagine that experience. As in all play, the rules—in this case, the elements of fiction—are what focus the play and help it to thrive. Consequently, it is essential for writing teachers to set in place supports that successfully nurture and balance play. The following section focuses on the precarious balance of play and structure with regard to writing fiction about real events.

The Problem of Writing What You Know

The rules for playing with real events in fiction might be summarized with the aphorism "Write what you know"—advice that advocates drawing exclusively upon the familiar for material. However, as Grace Paley states in the quote I chose to open this chapter, writers do not write what they know. Rather, "We write what we don't know about what we know" (Murray 1989, 106). Or, as Toni Morrison explains, "I'm just trying to look at something without blinking, to see what it was like, or it could have been like, and how that had something to do with the way we live now" (Jaffrey 2000). Working from this premise, Donald Murray (1989) says he encourages his writing students to start with a character, "probably drawn from those we know, but not too consciously" (108). Then, working with this somewhat familiar character, they can extend outward to a scene, as "character meets character" (108). Murray adds that once students begin writing, it is important that they move away from plotting out the story, but instead concentrate on *inhabiting* the story—writing fast enough to "enter the text . . . getting down what we are seeing and hearing and observing and, yes, experiencing" (111). They play in the story world, making that universe somehow real. Then, they return to the text and read and revise.

I return often to Murray's word *inhabit* when I teach writing, using it as a touchstone. The word derives both from the Latin *habitus*, meaning the practice of, and *habitāre*, to dwell. Inhabiting a home is different from simply living in it; rather, it infers a regularity, a daily practice of dwelling within the story world, a sustained experience repeated over time. The fictional milieu must be developed enough to shelter its writer—and later, its readers—for a lengthy stay. Like veteran travelers who bring their own pillows on hotel visits or who take along pictures of loved ones to set on a motel bedside table, writers make themselves more comfortable inhabiting the new world when they bring along a piece of the world they know. Or, to borrow from Stephen Minot (1998), writers necessarily "keep one foot in the circle of familiarity while reaching out with the other" (153).

Minot notes that this technique is especially important for beginning writers, who may feel that their lives are not interesting enough to be subjects for fiction. Nothing could be farther from the truth, as he explains:

> Using personal experience selectively and honestly is your best safeguard against work that is unconvincing. This is particularly true for those who are just beginning to write fiction. . . . Memories of a summer job on a construction crew, for example, might allow you to explore what it would be like to

be a foreman or, pushed further, a civil engineer in conflict with the foreman. Some of the more demanding moments of baby-sitting might serve as the basis for a story dealing with the life of a single parent. (153)

As Minot implies, it is the judicious, selective, and imaginative use of the real that persuades the reader to accept the fiction. Once grounded, the writer—and reader—can pull both feet into the imagined world. Now inhabiting that world fully, the writer can be tied less to what is known, and as Morrison puts it, imagine instead what could be. In contrast, when students produce writing that is uninformed by personal knowledge, such as in the following extract from Tim's story about a mortar attack, we find an increase in clichéd images and language:

> I woke up to a thunderous crash. It felt like an earthquake. Instantly I knew we were under attack by enemy mortars. I tried to walk to the window, and was thrown off my feet by a crash from a mortar exploding ten feet away. There was a tremendous pain in my cheek; I felt as if it were on fire. I ran down the corridor to the supply room, carrying my AK-47, like the rest of my regiment. One after another, the mortars were raining down like giant hailstones.

Without personal experience as a touchstone, and without pursuing additional research to compensate, writers like Tim necessarily draw on media—commonly, movies, gaming, and television—as substitutes for knowledge. While Tim may inhabit this story to some degree, it feels more like he is running through a videogame than creating and living in his own sustained world.

Writers pull back temporarily from their imaginary play during revision, when they necessarily put a foot back into the real world. They must consider the story from the reader's perspective, bridging the two worlds. As Langer (1995) explains, readers also seek to inhabit, or "envision," a text. They move around in the world of the text, staying in it for awhile, figuring it out by "asking questions about motives, feelings, causes, interrelationships, and implications" (17). During revision, writers necessarily anticipate this response by considering the whole effect of the story. The story has become a fiction in which events or people drawn from real life become blurred and changed by the text representing them and by the imaginative components that surround them. It has to work as a new world on its own—it has to have verisimilitude. Writers seek feedback on how much their readers understand and accept this new world; this provides the impetus to change or delete scenes—even those that really happened—and to add more fictional elements that transform the original elements further. At this point writers work in service of their art, paying allegiance to the story rather than its original lived inspiration. The story becomes its own truth, its own reality—and the writer shapes and crafts it to reveal its truths more clearly. This reshaping of allegiances makes revision a complex and potentially discordant enterprise, as writers come to new, potentially unexpected understandings about themselves and the world.

The Conflict and Payoff in Playing with Reality

Thus far, I've laid out the tensions in this kind of play as writing what you know versus shaping what you know into fiction. We could also call this achieving desires (or at least exploring alternatives) versus creating successful fiction. Here's how the conflict plays out.

Achieving Desires (Exploring Alternatives)

Think back to adolescence. You probably had turbulent relationships. You wrestled with fear, anger, regrets. You explored your boundaries—perhaps carefully, perhaps chaotically—feeling more than anything a life on the precipice of independence. Writing happens to be a particularly safe and effective way for adolescents to explore, control, and even push these boundaries further. The high school seniors in my project told me how fiction helped them in many ways—to gain a better self-image, to recover from their parents' divorce, to rebound from bad relationships, to imagine a more inclusive school culture. As Julia put it, "I think some pieces just need to be told for the author's sake . . . the author just really needs to say something."

Jack explained, "Sometimes when I'm feeling sorry for myself, I like to laugh at myself, so I write *Saturday Night Live* skits of what happened."

Brad used the safety of a personal poem to reflect on how conflicts with personal relationships push and pull his emotions:

Moot
because school acquaintances are fake
because you never answered "Why?"
I run and I skip and drive
until I pass your house again
bright house
once my house
my eyes cloud over with hot liquid
"I won't do this again!" I cry out
but I pull onto the gravel
and burst through the door . . . chipper
lovely
happy
completely not

In Figure 4–1, John lampoons a boring class in high school, finding writing material everywhere he looks.

In contexts less typical of my participants, children and teens may use writing to recover from more devastating events. National Book Award Finalist Patricia Smith (2008), who has brought poetry workshops to schools, community groups, and prisons, described what happened when she met Nicole, a girl who had just lost her mother to drugs. Contrary to Smith's expectations, Nicole did not want to write about her mother's death or about drug addiction; she wanted to write about her mother's singing. Smith observed that writing about this subject helped Nicole, because it gave her "something that was going to take her from one place in her head to a safer place: When you start writing poetry it's like having a second throat. Some of us go through our lives never knowing that throat is there." The "second throat" of poetry—not unlike the safe world of fiction—

Wind curls up the blinds in the window,
flipping them inside out, then outside out,
up and down, with rythum.
Twenty faces encase 40 eyes,
which wander around again and again,
bouncing off of each other.
Joey thinks about sex and
Courtney thinks about college.
An older women crosses the front
of the room, working hard on
her acting skills.
A dull voice filters in from
behind a wall, and seems
to complement the older woman's
perfectly; bored repetition overlapping
bored, faked repetition.
Karen is close enough to see
out the window, in between
gusts of wind, while the blinds
are horizontal and little
slots appear. The change of
pace only brings a new
flavor of boredom. The
actress shines as her
audience passes notes.

FIG. 4–1 *John's playful reflection on "bored repetition"*

provides a place for youth to achieve a desire, a memory, an alternate reality.

Creating Successful Fiction

Now imagine again that you're a teenager. You are writing a story in which the thinly fictionalized parents are arguing again, and the teenage daughter gets off the sofa in disgust, goes into her room, and slams the door. This writing is helping you to let off steam, and when you finish, you feel better. But when you share your story with a friend, you are surprised by a critique. Your friend says that it may be an important story to you, but it doesn't make very interesting fiction.

Let's hope that this imaginary friend is not quite as blunt as Kevyn, who simply said about a similar story, "You don't always want to read about things that are that trite." But Kevyn has a point. Real-life events do not always make for good fiction. When writers only write for themselves, without considering the expectations of their chosen genre or the needs of their readers, they are likely to produce melodramatic retellings or long episodes of banal conversation. "In [my] journals I can happily be my own hero and victim," playwright John Guare (1992) admits, adding, "But when you translate that journal material into a play, you begin building a new world; and the 'I' becomes just another citizen of that world to be treated with the same objective scrutiny" (99).

To use the events of real life as the basis for successful fiction, then, writers must take on a difficult task. As Minot (1998) put it, they must "establish control over the material and start thinking about it in fictional terms" (157).

The Payoff: The Opportunity to Do Both

Imagine the potential if students can learn how to use material from real life as fodder for successful fiction. As students satisfy their developmental desires to safely explore and play with real motives and events, they can also develop the skills and techniques that writers use. My research shows that students do not arrive at this balance easily. Rather, students often come to fiction with the mistaken belief that *real writers make it all up*. Witness the following assertions by project participants:

> I can't write about fake people. . . . I can't do it about a character I've never met before, just making this character that nobody's ever seen. (Michael)

> It's a creative writing class, so I figure you have to make a story out of the whole thing. (Susan)

> Everything that I write has been sparked by something that I did or affected me. So what I need to try to do is just do something totally different and just make stuff up, I guess. (Julianne)

What these students need is to find the payoff, to see how carefully selected details and events drawn from real experience give fiction breath and form. This is where our writers need help—not exclusively with exercises or formulas for stories, though these have their uses (see Chapter 2), but with instructional support that overtly addresses the relationship between the two worlds, the verisimilitude that grows out of well-anchored fiction. Author Julio Corazar put it this way: "I see a character, he's there, and I recognize someone I knew, or occasionally two who are a bit mixed together, but then that stops. Afterwards, the character acts on his own account" (Murray 1989, 109).

Tracking Four Student Writers

In the section that follows, I provide examples of two kinds of writers: those who were able, with the help of their teachers, to navigate a successful balance that enabled them to transform real events into workable fiction; and those who were less able to do so, whose fiction lacked authenticity. The problematic parts of their fiction exemplify the challenges we see in many early stories: unwitting telling, not showing; unplanned summation of scenes; transitions that move rapidly from one event to the next. Throughout I ask, "What helps—and hinders—a writer from inhabiting the story, and what kinds of writing result?"

To explore these issues, I selected two students who highly identified themselves as writers and who were motivated to seek out techniques that would help to craft their fiction, and two who strongly identified as nonwriters. I developed a series of measures drawn from interviews, surveys, and the teachers' assessments to see what affected these issues and whether there were any patterns in the instruction that appeared to help or hinder both sets of students. Interestingly, the one technique that appeared the most effective in helping students discover ways to play successfully in fiction was the writing workshop approach (Atwell 1987; Calkins 1986; Graves 1983). Though more than two decades have passed since the writing workshop approach was first popularized for elementary and secondary teachers, it remains a powerful pedagogy because it centers on techniques that support writers at play: self-generated topics, frequent peer and instructor feedback, sustained writing time, required revisions, and minilessons on craft that focus on particular skills and techniques. We'll see these features surface in the successful examples that follow.

The Teachers

Before we look at curricular influences on these four individual student writers, let's take a look at their writing teachers—Matt Phillips, Gail Goodwin, Jewel Fulton, and Winnie Hoffman—and their curricular choices.

Mr. Phillips

Matt Phillips' pedagogy was consistent with his vision of helping students become lifelong writers. Classes often included extended modeling by Phillips in the form of a story taken from his own life or related to something in the media, such as a National Public Radio program. Following this, he drew upon a writing workshop approach by reading something to students from a text on writing, generally using *Creating the Story* (Rule and Wheeler 1993); these examples served as minilessons on particular issues, including grounding a character, structure, beginnings, details, endings, revealing information, and point of view. Overt discussion of these issues or analysis of an exercise sometimes followed. (Of the four teachers, Phillips had the largest proportion of time for whole-class talk about writing.) Students then had unstructured time during a long block-scheduled period to write on their own topics or incorporate the lesson of the day. Phillips wrote along with them. He required students to hand in a long piece and a short piece of writing before the end of every marking period; each piece must have gone through revision and needed to include feedback from multiple readers. Consequently, classes also regularly included time for students to have one another read and react to their pieces, using response sheets for a general reaction and specific suggestions. Phillips distributed checklists that provided key ideas for the different genres in which students might choose to write, and he offered extensive teacher commentary on student drafts. Offering a checklist for revision and talking seriously to the students about taking risks with their revisions, Mr. Phillips suggested, "You may change everything around—and the first time you do it, it may actually plunge, but you won't let go of it . . . you are willing to take those risks and see what will happen."

Ms. Goodwin

Gail Goodwin designed her class to expose students to a range of genres, especially those with which they had little experience. Over the course of three months, the class moved through at least five projects, ranging in length from two days to four weeks—including a group comedy skit, a children's book, a poetry portfolio, a mystery story, and greeting cards. (The mystery story is discussed in Chapter 3.) Goodwin used her formidable organizational skills to take students smoothly through the wide range of activities. Alternating between teacher-directed activities and independent or small-group work, Goodwin focused on ways to engage students in writing and in sharing writing. In fact, sharing writing occurred in her classroom more than three times as often as it occurred in the other classrooms. At 7:30 in the morning, her first class of the day, Goodwin could be counted on to get students enthused about being in writing class. Although she engaged students in social conversation around the activities and encouraged them to share their own writing aloud with the class, Goodwin avoided much serious response or discussion about writing. This limited the effectiveness of writing exercises and sometimes confused students about their purpose. (I discussed her Mad, Soft, and Fast Talking activity, an exercise to develop voice, in Chapter 2.)

Ms. Fulton

The curriculum in Jewel Fulton's creative writing elective was designed to develop students' practice and understanding of writing techniques, primarily in narrative, with some exposure to poetry and memoir. Over the semester, students engaged in at least eight topics of study within the field of creative writing, including setting, essential features of narrative, character development, humor, poetry, plot, memoir, and poetry with narrative and plot. Recurring activities included writing original texts (individually or with a partner or group), discussing a topic or genre overtly, reading texts to learn about technique, and gaining information about writers' habits and behaviors. Fulton held an MFA in creative writing, and she told me that she wanted students to develop "tools they can use in their writing," presented in such a way so that they "can see the separate pieces that go into making a successful story" as well as how the separate parts "overlap and how they connect." For example, she had students watch the postmodern German film *Run Lola Run*, which explores multiple endings, as a means of talking about plot—how writers use it, what it does for a story, and how twisting the plot affects other elements of fiction. See Figure 4–2 for a sample of the thoughtful notes Fulton took as she watched the film, showing her commitment to having students really examine plot and its function in a comprehensive way.

Fulton's Character Bags activity, an exercise to develop characterization, is discussed in Chapter 2. Her students spent a signifi-

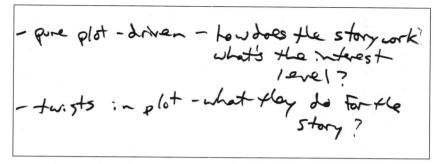

FIG. 4–2 *Ms. Fulton's notes*

cantly greater amount of time discussing writing and responding to one another's fiction than students in most other classes—two characteristics that fit with Fulton's approach to writing instruction.

Ms. Hoffman

Winnie Hoffman's students spent an unusual amount of class time writing—nearly twice the amount of time spent by the other students I studied. She organized her eight-week fiction unit around a number of short exercises designed to teach elements of fiction, including setting, characterization, flashback, and point of view. Once students finished this series of exercises, Hoffman assigned a full-length short story. Often referred to as "the newspaper story," the assignment involved selecting a news article and writing a fictional story that led to the events it featured. In advance of the writing, Ms. Hoffman asked her students to complete a detailed list of questions about the story they anticipated writing. (In Chapter 3, I discussed the tension this created for students.) Students had approximately two weeks, much of it uninterrupted class time, in which to draft the story. They worked individually with little discussion or peer feedback, although in one instance Hoffman asked students to comment on one another's introductions. Hoffman, believing that most students at this age were not ready to revise their writing, approached the course as a survey to offer students an exposure to a wide variety of genres.

The Students

In-depth analysis of the collected writings of four students in the project—Kurt, John, Roxanne, and Denise—enabled me to compare two higher-achieving students who identified themselves as writers (John and Roxanne) with two lower-achieving students who identified as nonwriters (Kurt and Denise). Overall, I found that those who were able to find and use real-life material for fiction—Kurt and John—showed the most growth as writers over the semester. Kurt, who did not self-identify as a writer, relied heavily on Mr. Phillips' supportive instruction to advance. John, who had significantly more writing experience and motivation, was able to advance with the help of just one helpful strategy, the topic generation search.

By contrast, Roxanne and Denise developed their fiction writing least. Yet both showed areas where they were successful: Roxanne, when she inhabited the world of her own experience while writing a memoir, and Denise, when she had the time and motivation to step into an imaginary setting and look around. In the following section, we'll explore each of these students' writing to see what their experience can teach us about the boundaries between real life experience and fiction, and the mediating factor of instruction on students' motivation to write.

Kurt

I was surprised to discover that Kurt's poor past achievement and attitude toward writing were mitigated by the writing workshop approach that Mr. Phillips, Kurt's teacher, used to support Kurt's in-class writing. Kurt himself ranked writing relatively low in his list of things to do, commenting, "It's not the thing I love to do most. So I don't know, maybe one day when I'm out of drawing paper and have no car to work on, then I'll write." This lack of interest showed itself in his writing during the semester whenever he was restricted to given prompts or to topics beyond his range of experience. In these cases, the texts lack elaboration and fresh language; they read more like summaries of television shows.

> The minister paused a minute, then said, "If there is anyone here that knows a reason why these two should not be joined in marriage, speak now or forever hold your peace." The groom held his breath, hoping there would be no outburst.
>
> Just as the minister was about to finish, a young woman burst into the church. She was in her late twenties, and had sandy blond hair. She was wearing an attractive red dress that left very little to the imagination. She came in yelling," Stop, I love you, you're making a big mistake! Please..."
>
> Everyone turned abruptly in disbelief. They saw that the young woman had been crying. And though she was attractive she was a mess. *Detail! Show that she's a mess*

FIG. 4–3 *Kurt's response to a prompt*

For example, a writing assignment for my study asked students to complete a prompt about a wedding. In Figure 4–3, Kurt writes, "A young woman burst into the church . . . she was wearing an attractive red dress that left very little to the imagination. She came in yelling, 'Stop! I love you. . . .'"

When Kurt had the option to write about events in his own life, his words rang truer, as in this description of the day he found out his family was moving across the country:

> I came in from swimming in the lake, and everyone in my family was seated around the dinner table. They were not speaking, and the looks on their faces were like none I had ever seen before. I could tell there was mixed emotions in them.

Although Kurt is writing at a level of abstraction—we don't see what the facial expressions are—we have the feeling that he is there; this event resonates for him.

In his response, Mr. Phillips suggested that Kurt might want to "tell it more like a story." With a captive audience of peer readers at the ready, Kurt decided to revise as suggested, moving these real events into fiction and giving them to a third-person narrator. This gave him that all-important distance and enabled him to release his concrete hold on actual events to play with them, changing them and crafting them for his readers. His resulting piece includes more elaborated scenes and descriptive detail. It's telling that it has grown four times longer. Here's an excerpt based on the scene shown earlier, now fictionalized:

> John came in through the beachside door. He was a thin, some would say scrawny, teenager. He had brown hair and was wearing a towel around his neck with green swimming trunks. He was still drying his hair as he walked in. Halfway in he realized he hadn't washed the sand off his feet. . . . His whole family was seated around the dinner table. They were all looking at him as he tried to hide sandy feet. He thought he was going to get in trouble, but instead of yelling at him, he parents told him to sit down.

Here Kurt is taking the time to let the reader dwell in the story, to see and feel what is happening—and even to foreshadow conflict through the sand on his feet. Kurt seemingly *inhabits* the scene, to return to Murray's word, staying with it and exploring its details.

For his final short story in the class, Kurt used the same strategy and fictionalized something he knew well, a football game, again using third-person narration:

> When the ball finally got to him, he received it as if it were an egg. He watched it into his hands, then carefully, but quickly, covered the nose of the ball with his middle and index fingers. The other end of the ball was jammed in his armpit. After he secured the ball, he turned to run upfield. Just as he turned he was met. There was no avoiding this one.

Mr. Phillips responded positively, writing on Kurt's paper, "I like how you take the reader inside the action of the game . . . and show moments that shape this character." Kurt's peers were also complimentary, recognizing that they, like the author, had become involved in the story. One wrote, "Many of us 'observers' of the game of football don't realize how emotionally charged some split-second moments can be." These responses must have been gratifying to

Kurt, who had told me that he liked to think about what was going on in the readers' minds as they read his work. In fact, he liked to play with what he thought the readers would expect, "Just to get the attention."

Receiving peer feedback as part of the requirements of Mr. Phillips' class became very important to Kurt as he learned how to refine his writing from a reader's perspective. In a telling reflection, he described his growth over the course of the semester in terms of audience: "Now when I write I look at it from [how] I think the audience or whoever's reading it should look at it or how they're gonna see it. So it's helped me make details more graphic." The extensive comments Mr. Phillips wrote to Kurt also supported his progress, for he often took this advice to heart in his revisions.

In group interviews, Kurt was often quiet, listening to others and offering an occasional comment on their remarks. Yet in our final group interview, when asked what he had really liked during the semester, Kurt spoke up first, saying, "All the free time to write." Later in the same interview, when asked what elements of the course should remain the same, Kurt again jumped in, suggesting that Mr. Phillips "keep the writing time." These comments and others like them suggest that Kurt valued the course because it gave him the time and opportunity to write "free" pieces that were meaningful to him. And in this way, he sounds like a writer, for time is what many wish for—extra minutes to play on paper.

John

A second student who benefited from the writing workshop pedagogy, John, had a very structured teacher, Ms. Goodwin, who nevertheless offered students the opportunity to use their journals as a place to explore writing ideas freely. The writing journal became a key element of John's writing development.

John was an advanced writer who reported that as early as fifth grade he was reading Gary Paulsen and trying to "copy his style . . . often [using] extended, run-on sentences." In one of the first required pieces for the class, a narrative about his past writing experiences, John wrote about his habit of looking at authors' writing styles as models for his own work. Yet his early journaling was somewhat dull—complete but lifeless. The assigned prompts were just about what you would expect by a teenager doing homework to answer prompts such as "describe a walk in the park."

During the second month of the class, Ms. Goodwin led a topic-search activity, offering a list of prompts designed to elicit memories and ideas in students, who simply jotted their thoughts in a list for future reference. For example:

- Writers set their stories in a specific place. I want you to jot down territories and places you know well. Think about images from those places, things in them. Jot them down in a list. Get as many down as you can think of.

- Writers also develop plot, which often grows out of particular conflicts. Write down, or list, relationships that have caused conflict for you, of some kind, or even on some conflicts that may be unresolved. You can change or embellish these in your journal.

- Finally, think about characters. Let's start with states of being—emotions—try to think of as many as you can, not just love/hate/anger. Then try to think of people you associate with those emotions. List as many as you can. This can become really good material for character development.

John told me that he had completed topic-search activities before but he had never returned to them afterward to find material for writing. This time, he marked the list with a star and the word *IDEAS* for later use (Figure 4–4).

After she offered the prompts for writing topics, Ms. Goodwin went one step further: She planted the suggestion that, in a writer's hands, the people we spend our time thinking about in the real world—particularly people who cause conflict—can turn into good possibilities for character development. She urged students to use their journals to explore details and people and places that could later become the foundation of a short story. Her focus on "people who cause conflicts" may be particularly appropriate for adolescent writers;

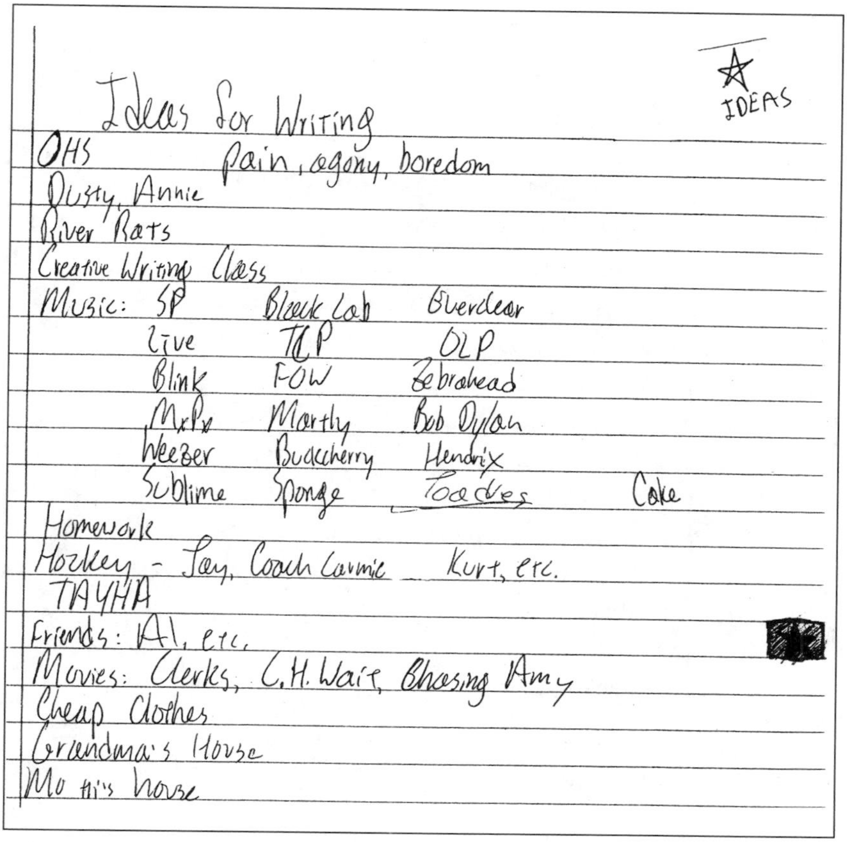
Ideas for Writing
IDEAS
OHS pain, agony, boredom
Dusty, Annie
River Rats
Creative Writing Class
Music: SP Bleeck Lab Overclear
Live TCP OLP
Blink FOW Zebrahead
MxPx Martly Bob Dylan
Weezer Buacherry Hendrix
Sublime Sponge Toadies Coke
Homework
Hockey - Jay, Coach Carmic Kurt, etc.
TAYHA
Friends: Al, etc.
Movies: Clerks, C.H. Wait, Chasing Amy
Cheap Clothes
Grandma's House
Mo thi's house

FIG. 4–4 *John's topic search*

Sarah, for example, made a lengthy list, which shows that adolescents have plenty of material to play with in fiction (see Figure 4–5).

Though Ms. Goodwin never specifically assigned students to use the list outside of their journal, John returned to it several times for inspiration, often using it for writing assignments in his other English class. He told me that although on the surface the list was full of nonfiction topics, he used the list for stories because fiction "can come out of the real stuff that happened." He noted that as he had "changed and grown up a lot in the last couple years," he was able to find more such sources for his writing. One wonders whether some of the growing up he had done was due to the writing he had practiced.

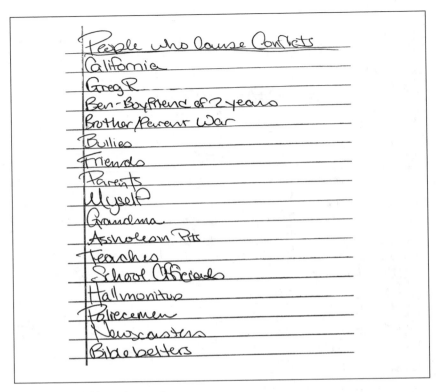

FIG. 4–5 *Sarah's topic search*

After the topic-search activity, John's writing became more developed; a voice emerged. For example, in a descriptive journal entry, John infuses the events with a particular perspective and includes unexpected, humorous details that change the piece and make it recognizable as fiction:

> I woke up around 11 thirteen or so and snapped on some boots. Found a dog and walked him.

Near the end of the piece, John writes about a recurrent character of his, a girl with strawberry-blonde hair. He develops a driving rhythm and style, and he marks the piece with his own original voice:

> Metaphor surrounded her so I asked and yeah, she said I been deep in poetry. Come in. OK and she got herself some coffee none for me because I prefer—well anything. And a milk-

shake it was because her Mom was at work and her Dad in Vermont. Strawberry milkshake and my strawberry-blonde girl. Dog in the backseat and a twenty in the wallet. Bring the day on—I'm armed and ready. Bring it on.

John used his strawberry-blonde character several times during the semester, successfully reducing the constraints on his fiction by incorporating at least one character that he already knew well. Later, he repeated this strategy by building on his experience working at a grocery store, which he used as a setting for his mystery: a market late at night. Because John was an experienced writer, he needed less teacher support than Kurt to make these decisions and adopt these strategies; the topic-search activity and the suggestion that writers draw from their own experiences were enough for him, and his personal goals for writing helped him simultaneously focus on craft and development (Adler 2007, 23–24).

What works, then, in helping writers like Kurt and John navigate the balance between crafting fiction and playing with reality? The following features provide scaffolding that support writers.

In a Nutshell: What Works
- Give students permission to develop their own writing topics out of experience.

- Guide students through activities such as a topic search that help writers choose appropriate topics.

- Provide an audience in the form of sharing and feedback from peers and teacher.

- Encourage students to work on multiple drafts in response to feedback.

- Offer students class time to write in a supportive, focused atmosphere.

In addition to offering these supports, provide minilessons on craft as needed to encourage students to take thoughtful, reasoned approaches to writing.

Roxanne

Like John, Roxanne characterized herself as a good writer who liked to write. Unlike John, however, Roxanne was never able to make the connection between her real-life experiences and well-developed fiction. Instead, she significantly improved her writing of nonfiction. In a reflection written at the end of the semester, Roxanne credited the class and her teacher, Ms. Fulton, for helping her write "with dialogue and just adding more characters in general," a technique that she felt improved the "boring" results of an early descriptive piece. She described her memoir as representing her best writing from the semester, explaining, "[I minimized] my descriptions but I also worked in some dialogue too." Her analysis is borne out in the work itself, especially the memoir, which is developed, thoughtful, and emotionally gripping. In the following excerpt, Roxanne describes her reaction to a telephone call in which she learned that she would be kicked off the crew team if her erg (indoor rowing machine) scores were not high enough:

> Crying, but with some weird sense of determination, I ascended the stairs to my room. I put on my unisuit, put my lucky fifty-cent piece that I always carried when we raced in its usual spot, and placed my locket around my neck. I headed downstairs where my parents questioned me about what had happened. I briefly told them through my quiet sobs. They hugged me and told me just to try and do my best. I walked through the kitchen, past my uneaten dinner, which sat, untouched at my place on the table, to the door that led to the basement. I made my way down the stairs and to the next room where my erg lay. I looked at it with great fear.

The specific details and description used here suggest that Roxanne was reliving the experience as she wrote it, trying to remember every piece of the scene, trying through her words to help the reader inhabit the experience also. The memoir was the culmination of Roxanne's efforts in describing real events, and it demonstrates growth over a series of such pieces that spanned the semester. In her early autobiographical pieces, she described various important places, including her room and her grandparents' house. However, she did not necessarily see these events like a writer might. She did not, for instance, broaden perspective beyond her own point of view. Rather, she seemed instead to be trying to capture the moments as they really happened. In an early interview, she gave several reasons for this. In response to the question, "What sort of trends do you see in your own writing?" she answered,

> Mine's description. I get into that. What I like to do, I just noticed this by doing those journals, every time, I like to take a personal experience and I get so descriptive about it, sometimes it's ridiculous but I just like to describe. I like using my own personal experiences, my history. I just love . . . it's so much more personal and easier to do.

In response to the follow-up question, "Do you use that and make it fictional or do you keep it real?" she responded, "Sometimes I keep it real. Sometimes I take an instance and then change it a little and make it fictional." For the most part, Roxanne's journal writing seemed to be composed of, as she described them, "little [stories]" that were "actually . . . real, something that happened."

Over the course of the class, however, Roxanne was also asked to write several pieces of short fiction and poetry. Her fiction in particular shows a striking difference from the level of investment and detail in her personal writing. Contrast the memoir excerpt shown earlier, for instance, with several lines from the beginning of an untitled short story revision:

> The news hit her like a hard smack in the face. The shock and disbelief of the whole idea was too overwhelming. Michele felt like a train that had just been derailed from a track she had intended to take for the next few years.

Here Roxanne shifts from a memoir piece bent on showing the reader what an experience was like to a fiction piece that instead tells the reader about a character, Michelle, whom we never really get to meet. In this piece, she is not reliving an experience in her mind; she is summarizing it. Why does Roxanne seemingly abandon her personal knowledge and instead rely on familiar clichés ("hit her like a smack in the face")? She is missing an understanding about how real events can help her imagine these fictional pieces, can reduce clichés, and can invite the reader to live in the story.

Roxanne's teacher, Ms. Fulton, used a curriculum that incorporated a number of approaches tailor-made to help Roxanne significantly improve her personal narratives: a sustained focus on workshop and revision, an encouragement to write in a variety of genres, and a stress on the use of dialogue and character development. Judging by her memoir, Roxanne did learn how to stay in a scene and explore it to the last detail. She just never learned how to play in a scene of fiction.

I've since wondered whether it was a lack of motivation or something missing from her instruction that created this gap. If Ms. Fulton had asked Roxanne to create a list of possible topics for fiction, drawing from her real knowledge—as John did—would she have been able to draw on lived details to help her envision a fictional scene as she was writing it? If her fellow students had talked about the choices they were making and which details they were fictionalizing, would that have helped?

Denise

Denise's work shows some of the same patterns as Roxanne's work—namely, a difficulty sustaining an imaginary world within her developing fiction. Yet Denise has much to offer us as teachers, if we can understand where she had difficulty and use that understanding to consider what kinds of writing approaches would support her development.

Like Kurt, Denise did not identify herself as a writer; though she did write poetry on her own, she claimed that she did not like to write, would definitely not seek writing as a career, and was undecided as to whether she was a good writer. For Denise, fiction was an exercise in frustration. After completing her first short story for the class, she indicated that the experience, if anything, had intensified her feelings:

> I hate writing stories. . . . I don't want to do it. I guess I have
> good ideas but I get so frustrated with myself when I write

because I want it one way but then it just doesn't turn out that way. I just have short sentences like "He did that. Then she said this." . . . I want it to sound more like a book. Not like a kid's book. That's the way it sounds.

Several weeks later, after writing a second short story, Denise reflected on her continuing discomfort:

I don't like writing stories very much. I'm not into very long . . . I mean, if you look at my poems, they're all short—I'm not into long poems, either. I like to get to the point. I don't like dragging everything out.

Denise's journal entries and poetry tended to support her assertion that she likes to "get to the point" by writing short pieces. Most often, she seemed to be using poetry as a place to record her feelings and emotions, frequently about true events in her life. For instance, when Denise described her poem "Senses: Feel," she wrote that it "was created by a true story of how my boyfriend and I got together. It was a fun poem to write and it made me happy to remember that special day." She described her poem "That Was All" as her most meaningful piece, because "the poem states what I feel about a certain person and I'm happy that he likes me for me." The poem itself gives the impression that Denise was trying hard to capture everything about the person and her feelings about their relationship with one another. Here is an excerpt:

> He's on his own today
> Watching him from inside
> Waiting for him to come in
> Heat escapes through the door
> There's a feeling of his presence
> As he sits down next to me
> Cold escapes his body
> Over taking the warmth of me
> Mixed feelings all around
> As I lean towards him, he smiles,
> Sending chill's [sic] down my spine
> Closer I lean towards him. . . .

Though she occasionally draws upon clichés ("chills down my spine") and tends to idealize the moment, Denise's narrative is built on honest language that, as Kirby and Liner (1998) describe, reflects the "words in [her] own head" (227).

While writing poetry, Denise is able to suspend the play of language and write the words that she means to say, but when she writes fiction, the play gets in between her intention and the final result. Perhaps her use of lived experience in poetry gives her a control over the language that is missing when she writes fiction. Denise interprets poetry as a personal form in which to express her feelings and emotions, whereas she sees fiction as a literary form in which to make up stories about *other* people and their lives. This genre classification, while consistent with the assignments given in Ms. Hoffman's class, negates the possibility that we've explored in the first part of this chapter—namely, that fiction can also be a place in which to write about personal experience, one that can provide the author with a different perspective on a situation.

Denise used poetry in a similar way to Roxanne's use of nonfiction: to record and explore real events by seeking to capture a personal moment. Both avoided this real-world knowledge in writing fiction. Denise's first short story was written halfway through the semester after a ten-week unit on poetry. Her teacher, Ms. Hoffman, preceded the longer assignment with a series of short exercises designed to help students work through elements of the short story. For most exercises, she gave students a preselected scenario. On the day of a flashback exercise, for instance, students began with a journal prompt that asked them to write about "the most important thing that happened to you last week." Later in the class, Ms. Hoffman said, "I sort of asked you to flash back into your past by thinking about the biggest thing that happened to you. Now I'm going to ask you to flash back into the past of John Anders, in which he is approaching a coffee shop and deciding if he's brave enough, strong enough, to open the door and go in." Though students had written about something from their own past, it must have been a feat to transfer their own knowledge into that of a middle-aged man in a coffee shop. Not surprisingly, Denise had real difficulty relating. Here is an excerpt from our conversation about this assignment:

Denise: I couldn't do it. I can't go flashback. I don't think I was in the mood to do it. I didn't see myself as him and think. I think I rushed through it and kind of made up a stupid story and tried to put it together and didn't really use past tense.

Mary: Did you understand flashback?

Denise: Yeah, I understand flashback. I can write it well because that's what I'm writing now. Basically the whole thing is from the past. It's almost all in flashback but I couldn't think of any problems in a coffee shop without making it into a real story and I don't think I was in the mood to do it. It probably would have been interesting but the setting wasn't very interesting so I couldn't write on it.

Mary: The whole thing of him walking into the coffee shop and you knowing what happened later [after the flashback], you had trouble filling in the—?

Denise: I can't fill in other people's stories. That's just really hard for me to do.

Denise's frustration of filling in "other people's stories" again points to her intellectual separation, reinforced by the activity, between writing a "real story" about an arbitrary fictional character and writing about one that relates to herself. Many students in the project shared the same belief, devaluing self-experience as too mundane for fiction, and seeing writers as privileged individuals who can pull stories out of thin air. Interestingly, Denise blamed herself for her trouble, saying she was not "in the mood," adding that the task is "just really hard for me."

In the full-length short story assignment that followed, Ms. Hoffman asked students to select a newspaper article and write a fictional narrative that led up to its main event. Denise selected an article about a woman who died after a car accident dislodged a bullet from a previous head injury. Though it sounds far from her own experience, she liked her choice because, in her words, "It's an easy topic to write about. My story is only three sentences. It has no detail whatsoever, so I can fill in everything." She took a risk and wrote the story from the perspective of the woman's male companion.

I find two things striking about this story. First, Denise's attention to detail and fascination with the story created rich description that initially pulls the reader into the story:

> I brought her inside and she was dazzled with excitement at the sparkling crystal chandeliers. The light struck the glass stones as a single white beam, then shattered into a thousand threads of color. The rainbow holograms laid to rest on the velvet upholstery. The chairs were the richest of red with virgin oak. The leaf engravings carved right to the veins which sustained life. We sat at our table. The seats welcomed us to sit, for they fit to our bodies. The vase on the table exploded with light as the flowers gave off the sweet perfume of spring.

Her description, though fanciful and exaggerated, has enough specific detail to suggest she was trying to inhabit the story world. We follow the narrator's senses as they move from looking at the engravings to feeling the contours on the chairs to smelling the flowers in the vase on the table. The pacing of the paragraph, designed to establish setting and character rather than to push the plot along, reinforces the author's investment in the scene.

The second striking feature, however, is that Denise's increasing frustration with the writing resulted in plot summaries that distance the reader by the end. Up against a deadline, she was unable to remain deeply absorbed in the text world, as is evident in this excerpt from the last pages:

> We decided to have a child. We thought everything would be perfect for the child. Eve was then back into the hospital having our first-born son. We named him Jeffery. We nestled Jeffery into a day care learning center, because he had had a brain cancer when he was born, and had trouble learning as fast as the rest of the kids. At seven years of age we lost Jeffery to the cancer.

Part of the problem is that Denise simply ran out of time. Clearly, the level of imagination shown in the first extract required a great deal of time and energy (recall Kurt's repeated praise of extended writing time as an important feature in his development). Having slowly developed the first five pages over ten days, Denise wrote the last five in one night.

Denise continued to follow a trend toward listing or summarizing narrative events in her second story, a fairy tale that she completed in one class period "just to hand it in and get credit for it instead of a zero." Again, in this assignment Ms. Hoffman sidestepped the possibility of asking students to write from personal experience, directing them instead to write a story based on two pictures selected from a magazine—a character's face and a place. Denise's story lacks elaboration. Although the pictures may have helped a more experienced—or confident—fiction writer, Denise was too conflicted about fiction, too rushed for time, and too unprepared to approach the assignment in a way that may have eased the transition and helped her to connect some part of herself to the story. Even a minor variation in the assignment, such as using a photo of a place she'd been before, or bringing in a picture of someone she already knew, might have helped, especially if it had been combined with more time for story development. Although one or two assignments in a writing class may not erase years of frustration with writing, students like Denise show us that even self-declared nonwriters can play. I recall her description of the chair with "leaf engravings carved right to the veins," and I see a writer in progress. Imagine what more she could do.

What Teachers Can Learn from These Students' Experiences

As teachers of writing—any kind of writing—we can see how engrained genre classifications are for students. Ask some of them, and they'll tell you: Expository writing means five paragraphs and a thesis and is not creative in the least. Poetry means rhymed couplets—or unrhymed verse that has no form or pattern. Fiction is creative and has no rules. Real life is real life, and fiction is fiction, and never the twain shall meet—unless you cheat.

The students we've just read about—and their many peers—need teachers not only to help them learn about writing fiction—and writing selves—but also to give them permission and instruction to bridge fiction and reality. They need teachers who will say:

> Okay, get out a piece of paper and number it from one to twenty. I'm going to give you a list of prompts to help you think of things you've experienced, people you know, and places you've been. These are materials—to be changed as needed—for your fiction. Then, I'm going to ask you to pick one or two to adapt into your first story. We'll have some discussions up ahead about how to fictionalize these so that you can let go of them as reality and make them credible for your story.

These students need teachers who will say:

> I've got Marie's permission to share her story with you all. She just workshopped a piece and heard that it's not realistic. Let's read it together and discuss what may not be realistic about it, and whether *it could happen* in the story world, and see what Marie plans to do with it. What makes a story realistic, anyway?

In Chapter 5, I combine what we've learned to rethink the creative writing classroom. I identify features that support and affirm the power of play—play with language, play with reality, play with fiction—and consider the boundaries and relationships that are necessary to ground the play, producing more successful fiction.

Building a Creative Writing Curriculum

5

In Chapter 1, we explored the concept of play as a metaphor for creative writing, using familiar examples from childhood, such as Peek-a-Boo, to show that play is guided by rules and shaped by particular boundaries. But the good thing—no, the truly wonderful thing—about teaching fiction writing is that teenagers also know how to play. They do it all the time—mostly quietly, even surreptitiously, when parents and teachers are not looking. Witness eighteen-year-old Johann's journal entry, a poem about an everyday household appliance:

Washing Machine

chumpa chumpa chumpa chumpa chumpa chumpa chumpa
chumpa chumpa chumpa chumpa chumpa chumpa chumpa
chumpa chumpa chumpa chumpa chumpa chumpa chumpa
chumpa chumpa chumpa chumpa chumpa chumpa chumpa
chumpa chumpa chumpa chumpa chumpa chumpa chumpa
chumpa chumpa chumpa chumpa chumpa chumpa chumpa
chumpa chumpa chumpa chumpa chumpa chumpa chumpa
chumpa chumpa chumpa crepa chumpa chumpa chumpa
chumpa chumpa chumpa chumpa chumpa chumpa chumpa
chumpa chumpa chumpa chumpa chumpa chumpa chumpa
chumpa chumpa chumpa chumpa chumpa chumpa chumpa
chumpa chumpa chumpa chumpa chumpa chumpa chumpa

Or these lines from Sarah's journal entry, a poem she wrote during a trip to a favorite coffeehouse: "Outside, the cold continues/A car shivers at the bold red light." (See Figure 5–1 for the whole poem.) Or the eighth grader who says she wants to learn how to write "good scenery" and then immediately tries it: "Trees looking dark and heavy with fear, for the night is here and we are all upon it." Or a posting in a school newspaper: "Whazzup4thacrew?"

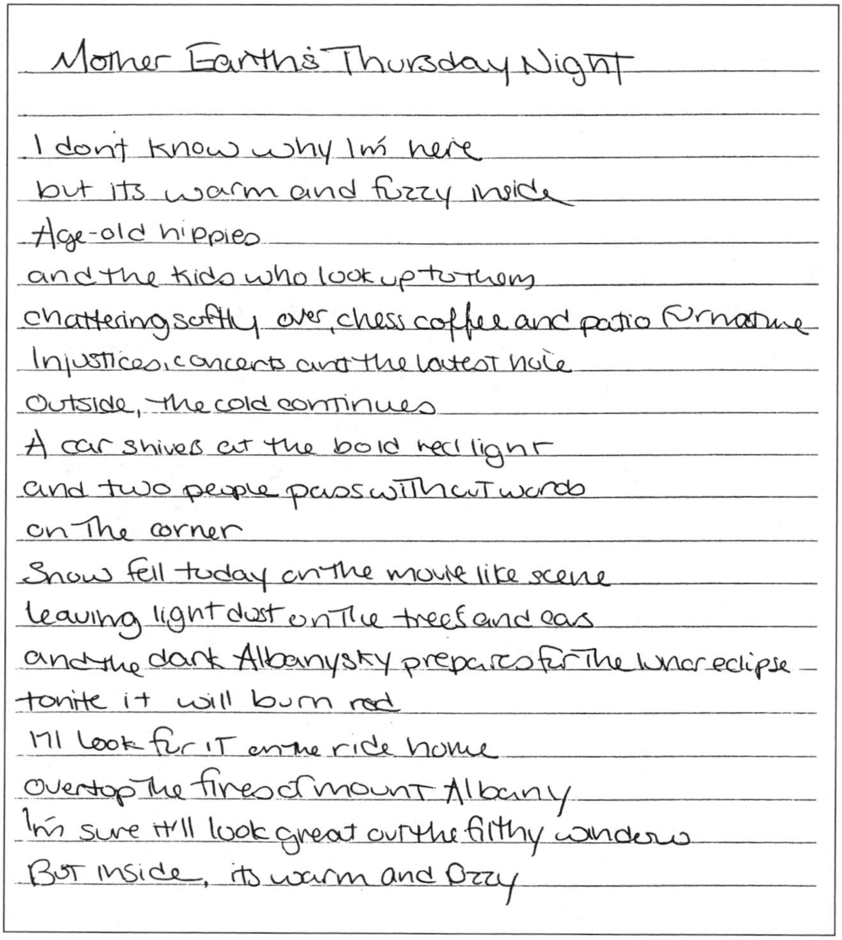
Mother Earth's Thursday Night

I don't know why I'm here
but its warm and fuzzy inside
Age-old hippies
and the kids who look up to them
chattering softly over, chess coffee and patio furniture
Injustices, concerts and the latest hole
Outside, the cold continues
A car shives at the bold red light
and two people pass without words
on the corner
Snow fell today on the movie like scene
leaving light dust on the trees and cars
and the dark Albany sky prepares for the lunar eclipse
tonite it will burn red
I'll look for it on the ride home
overtop the fires of mount Albany
I'm sure it'll look great out the filthy window
But inside, its warm and fuzzy

FIG. 5–1 *Sarah's poem*

Yes, adolescents play with both language and ideas—when they create text messages, as they sign yearbooks, when they invent stories and write poems. They play to explore language, to express humor, to reinvent what is real, to have some control over the formidable world that awaits them. This is good news for writing teachers! We do not have to teach adolescents how to imagine or how to be flexible with language, though we do need to give them permission to play, something that school has likely drummed out of them sometime around second grade. As writer Neil Gaiman (2009) told a class of seven-year-olds, "When I was your age, people told me not to make things up. . . . These days, they give me money for it."

What is more challenging for the writing teacher is this: We have to help teens learn how to channel both their linguistic and imaginative play into productive writing. In this context "productive" refers to writing that helps students realize their potential to connect, to reach readers, to create an effect on an audience. In short, we are after ways to help adolescents learn how to bring *us* into *their* imagined worlds. Thus far, much of this book has explored ways to do that: through initial writing exercises (Chapter 2), through revision strategies (Chapter 3), and through self-prompted writing (Chapter 4). In this chapter, we tackle ways to put these tools and strategies together into a curriculum.

Conceiving a Curriculum

The type of writing curriculum that you choose for your classroom will differ, depending on how you think about your students as writers. If you view your students as creative thinkers (but not necessarily writers), you might focus on creative expression, giving students opportunities to see the world through different perspectives (a lot of poetry, a little fiction, perhaps a children's book). Revision may not be a big feature of this class, if you're after play and experimentation with language.

If you think of your students as adolescents, who need to move out of their comfort zone in expository writing, you might develop a survey to expose them to different creative genres: memoir, short fiction, humor, drama, mystery, or science fiction. Here revision is more likely, at least in one major piece.

If, on the other hand, you think of students as adolescents but also writers in the long-term sense of the word, you're more likely to focus on developing a writer's sensibility: cultivating play in the midst of developing tools, techniques, and perspectives on writing. In the rest of this chapter, I'm going to focus on this last type of curriculum, because teachers with this focus seek the most development in student writing—and get it. However, the first two curricula are not faulty; choose a design that fits the needs of your particular students, or try out parts that make sense to you, as you continue to refine and shape your curricula over time.

Elements of an Effective Writing Curriculum

As mentioned, when you view students as teens *and* writers, you need to design a curriculum that helps them develop a writer's sensibility. Specifically, for this kind of curriculum you will:

- Focus on helping students find their own material for fiction at least as often as you focus on giving prompted writing.

- Provide models of texts to mine for writing techniques.

- Include time to practice and get feedback on some of those techniques.

- Focus on revision as an essential part of a writer's process, combined with frequent reader feedback and critique.

My research also helped me identify three essential characteristics of an effective writing curriculum, which we'll explore next.

A Sanctioned Place for Play to Develop

I use the adjective *sanctioned* rather than *safe* or *secure*, although those elements are important as well. Sanctioning a space for play implies approving of the play, supporting it, even creating a binding agreement that it may develop. In other words, students need some official (or semiofficial) recognition that this particular kind of play is permissible, encouraged even, in school so they may engage in the kinds of discussion and practice that are necessary for inexperienced writers to produce fiction. And they'll need to know that even in play, there is structure. There are boundaries. Imaginative play can be taken too far when the writers lose track of what is realistic for their story world. Linguistic play can, unchecked, ruin a perfectly good story. And making believe on paper can, without editing and feedback, lose the reader's interest or respect.

In Chapters 2 and 3, we saw ways that students and teachers help manage that play, such as creating goal-directed writing exercises, reflecting on successful ways to shape linguistic play while composing, and using mixed-media revision techniques that give the writer permission to play with alternative possibilities without losing the original text. Sanctioning play means more than offering playful writing activities; it means identifying, practicing, and applying this sort of management so that the play can benefit, rather than hinder or sidetrack, writing development.

A Chance to Discuss Practice and Review Models of Good Practice

Students need time and opportunity to reflect on their practice and to learn from one another's strategies and techniques. As we saw in Chapter 3, many students have created their own approaches to help them handle language play or solve problems as their fictional worlds grow more complicated on paper. These approaches are motivating to other students. More important, when teachers recognize students' existing strategies, they may avoid assigning new strategies (such as long lists of character traits to develop) that may conflict with the students' practices or needs. In addition, students benefit from examining models of good practice. These may be drawn equally from others in the same class and from published writers. For example, as one student explains how she punctuates dialogue, others may learn and apply the skill.

In my experience, writing models drawn from peers are more immediately effective with students than professional examples—this holds true from elementary school through college. The attitude with professional examples is "Of course he can do it; he's Hemingway." There is something so compelling about the immediacy of a classmate's good example (as opposed to the remote quality of a published, seemingly "authorless" work) that triggers an "Oh, I can do that" quality in the audience. Still, professional models are useful as exemplars, especially when students are trying a new genre or exploring a particular literary element (say, features of excellent characterization, or techniques in developing setting). Don't forget to include contemporary writers and artists that students see reflected in today's media. Figure 5–2 includes some favorite texts to use as models with students at varying levels.

An Established Connection Between Real and Fictional Worlds

Each of the creative writing teachers in my study assigned journals. While any sustained practice with writing is helpful, I've found that journal writing is particularly effective when students were asked to use it like professional writers do: as a source for developing ideas to test out in fiction, and as a place for posing questions to explore, sparked from real-life observations, societal and cultural critiques, and other texts. Teachers can support journal writing and other unstructured writing assignments by helping students look at their experiences as a jumping off point for writing.

One way to do this is to provide one or more topic search activities that support students in identifying ideas for fiction (see

Particularly good for plot/conflict:

Run Lola Run (film)
Sliding Doors (film)
Raymond Carver, "A Small, Good Thing"
Anton Chekhov (short stories)

Particularly good for language, voice:

Joy Harjo (poetry)
Rick Moody, "Boys" (rhythm, repetition, form)
Russell Baker, *Growing Up*
Sandra Cisneros, *The House on Mango Street*
Sharon G. Flake, *Money Hungry*
Student-selected song lyrics
Jamaica Kincaid, "Girl"

Particularly good for character:

Flannery O'Connor (short stories)
William Carlos Williams, "The Use of Force"
Sherman Alexie, *The Absolutely True Diary of a Part-Time Indian*
Richard Peck, *A Year Down Yonder*
Paul Zindel, *The Pigman*

Particularly good for considering description:

Tim O'Brien, *The Things They Carried*
Ernest Hemingway, "Hills Like White Elephants"
Annie Dillard, "Living Like Weasels" (from *Teaching a Stone to Talk*)
Gary Soto, *Baseball in April*

Particularly good for setting:

John Steinbeck, *Of Mice and Men; Cannery Row; The Grapes of Wrath*
Natalie Babbitt, *Tuck Everlasting*

Particularly good for point of view:

Wendelin Van Draanen, *Flipped*
Robert Cormier, *The Chocolate War*
Paul Fleischman, *Whirligig*

FIG. 5–2 *Favorite texts to use as models*

Chapter 4). Another is to suggest that students select one element from the story (plot, character, or setting are easiest) to ground with something they know. For example, when middle school students wrote stories after the Character Bags activity (see Chapter 2), I asked them to choose a setting that was appropriate for the characters and that they knew well—their school, their neighborhood, their local grocery store.

Enabling students to discuss how features of their lives can be intentionally transformed into fiction is a gift that they will take with them into the future, enabling them to continue to write even without prompts and exercises to stimulate them. Damien, for example, created his own "Brainstorming for Short Story" sheet, generating a long list of "Places I Can Write About," which seemingly could keep him flush with writing material for a long time to come (see Figure 5–3).

In Chapter 4 we explored what happens when student writers experience tensions between their need to write about their experiences as young adults and their desire to write "real fiction," which many assume means completely invented prose. The opportunity to figure out what it is that writers do with their fiction—and the recognition that writers, even published writers, pull from real life—is essential. Many young adult texts have interviews with the author as part of the bonus materials, providing an easy way for teachers to link the study of literature with the teaching of writing.

For example, in the reader's guide published at the conclusion of *Before We Were Free*, Julia Alvarez's (2002) novel about the political uprising in the Dominican Republic during the 1960s, Alvarez replies to this question: "In what ways did having a real, historical context make the writing process more difficult, and in what ways did it make it easier?" Her response would make an excellent lead-in to a discussion on the relationship between real life and fiction: "In actual fact, these two categories are often mixtures: What you've read, and what you know of history, and what has happened help structure the totally fictionalized story; and what you imagine and invent and embellish helps fictionalize the historical story" (173).

> Brain storming for short story   10/5
>
> <u>Places I can write about</u>
> Suburbia
> the Spectrum
> Altamont, Scotia, Dorothe etc.
> Staten Island, aka the shit hole
> The Jersey shore
> Private School
> Public School
> Comic bookstore
> Mall
> Book store
> Art store
> Sage Summer Art
> my "den"
> museum
> the lunchroom
> the internet
> GTA dinner
> pizzarea
>
> <u>Things I can write abo</u>
> Reading
> People watching
> going to the beach
>   " the movies
>   " the mall ~each
> Comics
> film
> being annoyed by my gen
> talking with friends
> GTA
> the virtue of a good breakf
> the lack of good pizza
> being a loner
> having a crush on someone
> hating someone irrationa
> ~~~~ ~~~~ listening to mu
> bickering parents
> forgetting something
> locking yourself out of the h

FIG. 5–3 *Damien's brainstorming list of material*

Other discussions of writing processes can be found in interviews or afterwords to novels, and numerous young adult authors have websites readily available, many with question and answer pages related to that author's writing process.

Regular Daily Features of a Successful Writing Class

Perhaps you'll use these ideas in a three- or four-week creative writing unit within a mainstream English classroom, or perhaps you'll apply them continuously in a creative writing elective. Perhaps you'll use them periodically in combination with literature study. Across any of these curricula, you'll have ongoing discussions—for as Arthur Applebee (1996) demonstrates, the curriculum itself functions as a larger conversation that grows over time. Within that big moving picture, though, you have daily snapshots—five lessons in most weeks—in which you regularly support your developing writers and readers. Consider incorporating (or rotating) several elements from the following list as regular fixtures in your daily lessons:

- *Writing time* (at least as much unprompted as prompted). This gives students regular opportunities to work through and develop topics and helps build fluency in writing. As Kittle (2008) points out, "The expectation that there will be time to write is important" (34). She describes how having a predictable writing time in her writing classroom allows students to plan ahead and rehearse what they will write, even hours ahead. In-class writing time also serves another useful purpose: It gives you time to circulate throughout the room and help students individually through brief conferences at pivotal moments in their writing development.

- *Student-generated sharing, questions, or observations about published writing.* If students are to learn about writing technique, they'll need some models to examine. For purposes of time, you might focus students on just a small piece of a larger text—a paragraph, an opening, a dialogue. This focused look will also help them to hone in on specific phrases and word choices. Resist lecturing about the passage; students' "aha moments" will be more powerful if they are the ones to discover what's working in a particular setting, how a character is developed, why a particular scene of dialogue is powerful, or why a plot twist surprises. Students may share their questions and observations briefly in pairs or small groups and then bring them to the whole-class. Once in the large group, the teacher can pose additional questions about the text and help students make connections between their ideas. Figure 5–4 provides a list of questions to get small or large groups started.

- *Sharing and feedback of students' own writing.* You will need to establish or revisit ground rules for feedback before beginning peer response (see Chapter 3). I like to have students meet with a few trusted peers to share their work, and I encourage them to stay with the same group for some time. That way they become familiar with one another's pieces and better at making connections across drafts. Some students—in middle school, high school, or college—are reluctant to share their work. This poses problems in a writing class. Jewel Fulton tackled this issue head-on the first day of class by providing a syllabus that stated, "There is no such thing as perfection, and you cannot 'write for yourself.' If you wish to simply write for yourself, you should not be in this class." She went on to note that students have "a responsibility as readers to assess the piece and offer sincere criticism."

  Peter Elbow (1998) reminds us that it's important also to have some sharing and celebrating time, in which students simply read a piece aloud and receive applause or thumbs up signs but no critique. Sometimes, the chance just to listen and really hear a piece, without an expectation of response, inspires most. Even sharing sessions held once or twice a week can enrich your classroom culture.

- *Reflective writing and/or discussion.* This can even be done quickly, on an index card that students give you as a "ticket out," so that students can articulate, for themselves and one another, what they have observed, learned, and discovered in writing or reading a piece. Use them to enhance your planning for the next day.

- *Brief exercises that provide scaffolding for new or difficult writing tasks, as needed.* For example, students may develop sentence

Select questions that relate to your purpose and the particular text

- Look at the first sentence. What does it tell you? What promise does it make? What does the writer accomplish with this sentence?

- Look at the last sentence. Does it relate to the first? In what way? What has happened?

- Who is telling this story? How do you know? Are there other possible narrators or points of view?

- What conflict is revealed so far? How do you know? What does this tell you?

- Whose story is this? How do you know?

- Tell me about the character you know best—what do you know about him or her?

- How do you know that? What details show you? What do they mean?

- How about the character's appearance? What does the character look like? What does that tell you?

- What about other characters? What do you know about them? When are they introduced?

- Are the characters likeable? Why or why not?

- When you write, do you try to create likeable characters? Why or why not?

- What is described in the story? How? What isn't described? Why not?

- A lot of people think this is a _____ (happy, surprising, creepy, etc.) story. Why might this story in particular _____ (enchant, surprise, bother, etc.) people?

- Where does the tension come from in this piece?

- What happens to the conflict by the end of the story? Is it resolved? How? (Or why not?) Are there other ways it might have been resolved? Why didn't the author go with one of those possibilities?

- What do you most admire about the author's work in this piece? Why? Jot down any favorite lines in your journal.

These questions focus students on the writer's work rather than on a literature analysis, which they are more used to doing. The questions can be easily adapted for any story at reading levels ranging from grades 6 to 12.

FIG. 5–4 *Writers' questions for any text*

© 2009 by Mary Adler, from *Writers at Play*. Portsmouth, NH: Heinemann.

variety by working with sentence combining. Perhaps they take four sentences that could serve as the lead for a story and combine those sentences in several different ways, testing out different rhythms, sentence lengths, and clause patterns. For each exercise, teachers should invite students to share their results and articulate any strategies that proved helpful.

- *In lieu of other scaffolding, an examination of a short piece of student writing for analysis and discussion of what works.* I rarely, if ever, use pieces as negative examples—there's not much to learn from what isn't working, and who wants to be the one on the chopping block? Using positive examples minimizes the fears that some students inevitably bring with them to a writing class, while encouraging risk taking, sharing, and community.

Teaching Students to Write Full-Length Short Stories

Many writing teachers, especially those that do not teach elective classes, include a unit around a single short story that is taken all the way through the writing process. That is, students generate a story concept, brainstorm various components such as characters and plot, produce a draft, revise for content, and then edit before handing it in for a final grade. In these cases, various kinds of activities and scaffolding will serve best at different points. Here are some suggestions to take you through the entire process.

Timing

Resist offering students a large list of character traits and plot points to complete prior to writing their story. At the beginning, students will need some limited scaffolding (mostly talking, journaling, and brainstorming) to step into the story, without overpowering their initial development. *Wait until midway through the process to offer more,* for at that point students may be ready to stop and reassess what they know about the story, what they need to know, and where they are headed. Save editing until after a draft has been completed.

It's too hard for students to hold the developing story *and* new editing skills in their mind at the same time.

Skills Exercises

Offer these *selectively and purposely* at key points in the process, when they are most relevant, and when students' writing warrants them. For example, a lesson on description may be helpful early to midway through, when students are crafting their characters. By contrast, a lesson on using strong verbs may be best saved for revision, after the flow of the story has been drafted and students are more ready to look closely at language choices. Whichever writing skills you teach, it's best to keep them minimal and use them repeatedly over time until students can do them independently, then move on to new ones.

Supporting Play Throughout the Process

Early On

Give enough structure to generate productive play in students' stories without overwhelming it with rules. Remember that when students are involved in creating narrative they need the flexibility of play in developing meaning, but for their stories to be successful, they also need to think like writers, maintaining the consistency of the story world in order for the reader to find it comprehensible (Bruner 1990). Here are some activities that work well at this point:

- Topic searches to develop ideas for writing (e.g., topic-search activity, Chapter 4).

- Exercises for character development (e.g., Character Bags exercise, Chapter 2).

- Model stories that the class examines for insight into how "they do it," especially with regard to developing conflict early on (e.g., writers' questions for any text, Figure 5–4).

- Practice with writing leads. Donald Graves (1989) has an excellent list of sample leads to study, from books by children's authors, in the slim but powerful *Experiment with Fiction*—don't be put off by the K–5 designation!

- Support in describing a setting (e.g., sketch the setting first, use a chart of the senses to capture it, or describe it to a friend who has never been there).

- Suggestions to build fiction from at least one known element, drawing from real life as the starting point for a character, a setting, a conflict, or a time period.

- Sample starters as literacy support. Offer these only to students who really need them; I sometimes include sample starters at the bottom of the page in small print. When I'm circulating about the room and I find a student who is stuck for a starting place, I point to the sentence starters. This usually helps the writer get the story going. For example:

  It was a _____ day when (name of your character) ran inside the (name of setting) and demanded to know . . .

  (Name of your character) had never heard that sound before, but as (he or she) turned around in (name of setting), (she or he) knew exactly what it was . . .

  (Name of your character) had already decided (something) when (he or she) saw . . .

- A word bank (that gets added to over time) for needed words/ phrases.

Midway or Mostly Through First Drafts

At this point you may want to provide some structural analysis and development techniques to give the writers more control over the developing play. Middle school students are likely to need this to happen a bit earlier than high school students. I like to give students a "ticket out" the day before we work on structure and development techniques. The "ticket" is usually an index card or half sheet of paper; I ask students to jot down their name and what kind of help they need with their draft: plot, character, setting, overall feedback, or something else. As students leave, they hand their cards to me, and then I quickly read through and group them by similar issues. When they come in the next day, they get into their assigned groups and I visit each group to give them a focused assignment. I find that these groups work well together because the students are motivated to explore their identified area. Some possibilities for group activities include:

- *Plot analysis*: Have students work with their developing plot. One way is to have students read their story aloud, one at a time. As the reader gets to a new plot point, he or she stops reading, thinks out loud about what has happened in the plot, and annotates that event in the margin. The rest of the group listens and speaks up if the author doesn't catch something or if there is a difference in interpretation. After the group has finished, students can rewrite their annotations as an outline. Or they might, as Linda Rief (2007) suggests, use post-it notes to draw the elements in a story-board format. The post-its can be rearranged easily as the writer experiments with new possibilities.

- A different way for a group to tackle plot is to have students each read their story aloud to the group. After it's read, the author asks the group to help identify the beginning, middle, and end of the story. A horizontal line is drawn after the beginning and just before the end. This process is less intricate than annotating, and easier for younger students, yet it still helps the writer visualize the progression of events. Sometimes just revisiting those—and helping others do the same—can refocus a writer to figure out why an ending doesn't work, or how a new beginning might be inserted.

- Yet another way to help students work with plot is to ask them first to read their story to their group and then to pose a series of specific questions related to plot, while another group member takes notes on what is said. Questions may include the following: (1) Tell the author what is happening thus far in the story; (2) What do you expect to happen next? Why? (3) What questions do you have about what has happened? (4) What promises do you feel the story has made? The written notes will help them later on, when they've forgotten some of the detail of their peers' responses.

- *Character development*: Have students take some time to revisit a central character or select a character who is turning out to be important but who is not developed. Ask them at this point to consider that person's character traits, write a back story for the character, or answer questions and brainstorm about the character with a partner or small group. The group does not need to have read the story to ask the author these questions and provoke interesting answers; in some ways, it's better if they haven't. Some questions might include: (1) What does your character look like? Dress like? How does he or she move? (2) What do you know about your character's past? (3) What does your character want in this story? Why? (4) What does your character know that nobody else in the story does? (5) Who do you know like this character? How are they alike?

- Sometimes students need to learn more about how to develop a character in writing—the technique of revealing characteristics through dialogue and description. In that case, a model is helpful; have the group read an excerpt and complete a chart like this one:

What we know about the main character	How we know it (description, dialogue, actions, things said about him or her)

After completing the chart and discussing the character, the students can take the right-hand column and test their own main character against it (Have they described him or her? Showed personality through dialogue? And so on).

- With middle school writers, I find it helpful to have students draw their character so they can visualize him or her moving through the story. In a small group, they might trade papers and have someone else draw their character, perhaps labeling the drawing with particular characteristics. This will tell the author how their character is interpreted by the reader—adjustments can then be made.

- Once their group discussions are finished, high school students might find an internal monologue useful, in which they write a long stream-of-consciousness commentary from that character's perspective. They should write it quickly, using the power of freewriting to stimulate language play and lead the author to new realizations.

- *Setting*: Ask students to trade papers and sketch the setting their partner has laid out in their story. Where do they need or want more description from their partner? Ask students then to take highlighters and go through their own story, marking spots where they could add description to the setting. For homework, they might visit a place that is similar to what they've used for the setting, by visiting it in person or virtually through the Internet or magazines. What details can they add to make it really sing?

- *Overall feedback from the teacher and/or another reader*: Ask students to pair up, exchange papers, and provide the following to one another (or you can read a piece and provide this feedback relatively quickly): a sentence summing up what the piece seems to be about; a real question they have about the piece; a specific compliment; and something that they predict about the ending. If students place the feedback on sticky notes, writers can put the notes next to them as they work. Also, because the comments aren't marked over their words, it doesn't take ownership away from this fragile world that they're building.

- *Minilessons on skills*: Frequently, students struggle with skills such as paragraphing, punctuating dialogue, consistently using the present/past tense, or shifting points of view. Depending on the size of the group needing help, you might even teach a minilesson on one of these skills to the entire class, and ask students who struggle with it to concentrate on that skill during their drafting and revision. (It's particularly useful if one or more students who use the skill successfully can model how it works.) This focus helps students internalize the skill and makes it more likely that they will attain its use (as opposed to correcting a variety of errors in a final draft). As time goes on, integrate the skill into other lessons when possible, to increase the potential for students to examine and use the skill over time, in different contexts.

- *Time for writing:* Invariably, when students complete their tickets, a few will tell you that their story is coming along—what they need is the time to keep going. It's a precious gift, especially for students who can't or won't write at home. So one group of students may sit silently writing, using the time to their best advantage.

After a Draft Is Completed

Peer Feedback

For writers to play successfully, they need to hear from their readers about what is working, what is confusing, what is included that should be removed, and what is missing that should be included. Mainly, they need to imagine a reader and step into that reader's perspective. This stimulates a different sort of imaginative play (in this case, leaving their own point of view temporarily behind and entering that of the reader). More directly, it increases the students' understanding of the limits or boundaries on their fictional play. If the fictional world of their creation—or the language they use to describe it—is not working for readers, they need to revisit and even reshape it. There are a number of ways you can orchestrate the feedback sessions. Here are two:

Informal Feedback

One of the teachers in the project, Matt Phillips, used a feedback format that works well for high school students. Before students submitted each piece for a grade, they were required to have two readers answer two general questions on a form (see Figure 3–11, on p. 87). Students appreciated the flexibility that allowed anyone to fill in the forms, not just classmates, and although they usually depended on classmates for feedback, they sometimes relied on parents or other relatives for critique as well. They also turned a draft in to Mr. Phillips for ungraded feedback. This was time-consuming for the teacher but very motivating for the students, who seemed most enthusiastic about revising before their work had been "judged" with letter grades.

Formalized Feedback

I have students meet more formally in class, in groups of three, to share their pieces before their final drafts are due. (This works for both middle and high school age groups, as well as college.) Before they meet, I ask them to select several questions that they have about their work, and to write those questions at the top of the page to ask their group. In his helpful book *Writing with Power*, Peter Elbow (1998) has an extensive list of possible questions that can be asked during peer feedback sessions. His reader-based feedback is adaptable to fiction writing and can easily be made into a handout. I have adapted some questions slightly for this purpose:

- What was happening to you as you read the opening passage? What were you thinking about?

- What words or phrases struck you most or stuck out or had resonance?

- What changes occur in your thinking as you continue to read?

- What do you expect next in the plot? What do you need before it ends?

- Summarize the story: Give your understanding of what it says or what happened.

- What is this story about? And what is it *not* about?

- Describe the narrator's relationship to the reader in terms of distance. Close? At arm's length? Distant?

- Use camera metaphors for how the writer handles the story. Where does the camera move in close, and where does it fade back? Where is it sharp or fuzzy? What is the foreground and background?

An alternative is to have students help you generate a list of potential questions to ask about their stories (Which character do you sympathize with most? What needs more description? and so forth). Students love these sessions and I find it really helps them write for an audience that includes their peers rather than simply writing for the teacher.

Revision

It's logical that after writers receive feedback, they will want to make some changes to their pieces in order to connect more meaningfully with their readers. Figure 5–5, for example, shows the feedback that a student named Lydia received from one of her peers. In response, she changed her opening to address the reader's request to "elaborate also on the setting" (see Figure 5–6).

In Chapter 3, I encourage the use of mixed-media revising, and I want to mention that again here, for it helps students play with possibilities—otherwise known as potential changes—without committing to any permanent moves. For this reason, having students simply type over the latest version of their story is counterproductive. Students are likely to fear global changes and they will also be unable to visualize the whole of their story, resulting in minor additions or deletions at the word or sentence level.

Instead, give students permission to play with the text. Have them bring in a one-sided copy of the story and model revision strategies (or, better yet, ask a student to do it). Draw right on the printed copy, using arrows, sticky notes, and symbols for additions completed on a separate page. After the revision process is finished, ask students to write you a paragraph about what changes they made and why. Sharing these in class, accompanied by brief "before and after" readings of paragraphs or sentences that were changed, helps to celebrate revision, provide models for novices, and create a culture where the hard work of reshaping play is celebrated.

elaborate on the setting also {

I'm sitting in that infamous purple sofa with a coffee cup in one hand and a pen in the other. It's a Saturday night and I'm listening to the musician who is playing guitar over in the corner. There is something about drinking coffee and listening to live music. It makes me feel warm and fuzzy all over. Or maybe that's just the coffee buzz kicking in.

I remember one time when I was at work and falling asleep. I rushed down the stairs to the little coffee shop on the corner and asked for the strongest brew they had. Let me tell you. I don't think I have ever been so wired in my whole life. I remember when I got home that evening my hands were still shaking. That was one heck of a coffee buzz.

elaborate a little more this about woman. {

I look over at the women singing with her guitar. She is wearing faded jeans, a wool sweater, and a pair of clogs. Her short, brown hair falls loosely around her face. She is not the kind of women who would turn heads. Even still, I look around and see everyone in the coffee shop staring at her in awe.

Perhaps it's the way she leans her head back and pours her heart and soul out. Or maybe it's the way she makes her songs come to life. But the real reason is that she has flaws and she is not afraid to show them. She knows she is not beautiful. She realizes that she will never make it to Broadway. Most importantly, she accepts herself for who she is.

FIG. 5–5 *Peer comments on Lydia's draft*

It's a Saturday night and I'm snuggled in the big, purple chair sipping my coffee and reading a book. I hear the clang of the door. A group of guys come in. They look like carbon copies of each other with their identical Abercrombie hats and jackets. They saunter over to the counter and order their drinks.

I watch as the built-up, blond guy tries to get a date with the girl making their drinks. He shoots out a one liner that goes something like, " Was your daddy a baker, cuz you sure got a nice set of buns." The girl behind the counter laughs at him. I feel pity for him, but then I come to my senses and let out a little laugh too. It's fun to watch guys stumble all over themselves trying to impress girls.

The group of guys, now feasting their eyes on me, has settled down at the table across from me. You can tell be looking at them that they don't frequent coffee shops very often. They must have come here in hopes of meeting chicks.

FIG. 5–6 *Lydia's response to peer comments*

Editing

I hold with the school of thought that separates editing (the correction of mechanical errors) from revising (the rethinking of story elements and language). I suggest being very selective in your editing work with students. You don't want to kill the spontaneous play with excessive editing. Yet for students to communicate their play successfully to readers, they need to become proficient in proofreading their work. Decades of research into key features of successful editing tell us the following:

1. Don't try to have students fix all or even most of the errors in the piece.
2. Focus on asking students to take responsibility for the fixes, not the teacher.
3. Use student-generated examples and explicit discussion of those examples as often as possible.
4. Return to these errors over time in other kinds of writing, to provide further practice.

Depending on the kind of class you have, one of the following approaches may be appropriate:

If you have a heterogeneously grouped class, chances are there will be pockets of students who have similar sorts of editing problems. Collect the students' stories and skim through them, putting them into piles by needed skills: paragraphing, sentence boundary problems (run-ons, fragments), comma usage, and so forth. Quickly identify the areas needing work with a wiggly line or a highlighter so students can find and fix them. Students who do not need help with mechanical skills can be grouped to improve other features of their language use: descriptive language, strong verbs, active voice. Put three or four papers in each pile and place a sticky note on top of the pile with directions for the group, such as *Your group needs to work on comma usage. I've attached a sheet with a few basic comma rules. Pair up and read over the highlighted areas. Fix the commas in those areas, then share with each other and see if the other pair agrees. Let me know if you get stuck.* Circulate to help clarify problems. When groups finish, ask them to share with the class for thirty seconds, reading something they changed and telling why they changed it. These whole-class discussions bring the conversation to everyone's awareness, and they hold each group accountable for being on-task. Chances are these group sessions will not resolve the issue, but they will keep it top of mind, and you'll have opportunities as you circulate to talk with students about ways to correct their language in the context of a meaningful story.

If you find that a majority of the students are having problems with a similar skill, prepare a five- to ten-minute minilesson. Select two or three of the students who do it well and ask them for permission to share their work with the group. Then put it on the overhead or have the students copy a sentence or two on the board. Ask them to describe why they edited it that way: *Why did you put commas here and there? Why did you use a semicolon here?* Ask the class to help generate a rule that fits. Then give students time to find those particular errors in their stories and fix them, checking with a partner. Circulate as they do this, and select a couple of students who have succeeded to put the "old" and "new" sentences on the board and share.

Publishing

Otherwise known as Audience! It's often said, but worth repeating: The teacher just cannot be the only one to read the students' pieces. The opportunity to test out writing for an audience, including peers as well as parents and the teacher, provides both novice and experienced writers with the chance to see how others make meaning from their words.

Another way to develop audience is to hold readings. There are numerous possibilities, depending on your time and resources. Have students sign up to read their piece and select one or two at the end of each day's lesson; have students read one anothers' work silently in groups, then trade papers and read another set, continuing until each group has read every other group's papers (in the read-around group approach, papers are anonymous and provided with a code number so that top papers can easily be identified for praise); or allow students to post their stories on your website, if available.

As a variation, I like to hand out whiteboard markers to students as they walk into class, and ask them to write their first and last sentences on the board, with ellipses between them. For the story I'm working on now, it would look like this: *The traffic took its own sweet time but finally cleared and I pointed my feet toward the coffee shop and marched across the parking lot to meet Dad . . . I'd have broken it if I could.* After students post all of the first and last sentences, I read them aloud. Then I ask the class for nominations to select a full story to be shared with the class. In addition to generating an instant audience, it has the added virtue of increasing students' awareness of the importance of beginnings and endings—and the relationship between the two. And, it celebrates the play, the inventiveness, the spontaneous leaps of thinking and surprising juxtapositions that make us laugh, make us think, make us leave wanting to write.

Denouement: In Which We Revisit the Beginning and Imagine the Future

Early in this book we explored two student-generated metaphors: the idea of focused freedom and the image of a bubble of air containing ideas. To this I added the metaphor of play as a way to think about what happens during all writing, and fiction writing in particular. As I think about how to end this book, these metaphors come back to me, still fresh, still appropriate, still provocative. They urge us to think of our teaching in spatial, even geographic terms. If the writing curriculum or even each assignment is a space living in the mind, then into that space we give students permission to enter, to walk (or jump or hop) about, to feel safe, to invent and play, to learn about its walls and doorways and the customs of those who have used the room before. Within the room there is oxygen to sustain and support the writing life, but not so much that students hyperventilate in anxiety.

What these metaphors we started with do not neatly capture is how this work of writing happens, and that is what we have been exploring in the intervening pages. I use the word *work* intentionally, for play is a challenging business, its players quite intense as they build and rebuild their imagined worlds. So, another way to think of the metaphor is this: When students have the freedom to write from the heart, from the imagination, from experience, *they are willing to focus.* They are willing to learn and apply the rules that enable their play to reach and inspire a reader. When they have a bubble of air to help them focus and shape their ideas, they breathe deeply.

In more concrete terms, play is harder to pin down (and doing so, in some ways, makes it seem less like voluntary play and more like a requirement). But we've explored several ways that teachers can open their awareness to play as it affects the writing process, particularly for adolescents. First, though it may be obvious, I encourage *you* to play. Try out some of these exercises yourself, even if you don't consider yourself a writer. Share a piece or a paragraph with students now and then. Let them see you struggling with a paragraph or an idea. Tell them about an experience that you're thinking of writing about; invite them to help you transform it into a seed for fiction or to find a starting place for nonfiction.

For your students, try out some of the lessons in this book, or apply the considerations raised in these chapters to the writing exercises in your filing cabinet. As you plan your semester, consider ways to do one or more of the following:

1. *Stimulate imaginative play.* Offer motivating activities that stimulate play and imagination. Consider using tactile objects, film scripts, role playing, what ifs. At the same time, you'll need to set boundaries for the fun entertainment by engaging students in discussions about the purpose of the activity and any products that

will come from it, so that they can make in-the-moment decisions that will help them discriminate between productive choices and frivolous, distracting ones.

2. *Stimulate language play.* Provide freewriting opportunities, especially early in the writing process, in which students can experience and benefit from ideas that grow exponentially, word to word. At the same time, you'll want to engage students in reflective discussions about what happens during these writing sessions, and how they can apply strategies such as note taking, outlining, annotating, or dialoging to recognize what the freewriting has produced and take advantage of it.

3. *Equip students with writing behaviors.* Show them how writers play: how to develop their own ideas for writing, how to listen to readers' feedback, and how to examine what other writers do, learning from professionals as well as their peers.

And finally, encourage celebrations, small and large, because that glorious feeling of successfully sharing one's play is rare and wonderful. We know that students' enjoyment of writing and their sense of themselves as writers starts out strong in elementary school and then gradually declines every year from middle school to senior year. Reinventing English class as a place to play with language, ideas, technique, and experience is one powerful way to reverse this trend.

Book Study Guide

Though primarily designed for discussion study groups, the questions below may also be used by individuals to reflect on the teaching of writing. Readers are encouraged to keep a journal of their reflections and to build on it over time, both during and after reading.

It's generally best to begin discussions with your own notes, questions, and ideas. You can use the following questions as it suits your group's intentions. These can be followed in order, or a few can be selected to stimulate deep thinking.

Introduction

1. What have you found to be the benefits of teaching creative writing? What social, cognitive, and/or personal growth have you witnessed in your students?

2. Discuss the kinds of writing taught at your school. How often is imaginative writing assigned? In what grades? How can you work together with colleagues to integrate creative writing more fully across grade levels?

3. Consider Jasper Neel's assertion that students who explore ideas in writing use language play to change from a "finite, knowable 'self' into another text" (1988, 132). What does it really mean to use writing to learn about oneself? How has writing helped you gain new insight about ideas, relationships, or life experiences?

4. Are you a writer who teaches, a teacher who writes, or somewhere in between? How does this persona influence your approach to teaching writing?

Chapter 1

Exploring the Forces at Work During the Creative Writing Process

1. Discuss the notion of "focused freedom" or "creating a bubble" for writers. As a teacher, how do you navigate between providing structure (e.g., boundaries, limits) and freedom (e.g., students' ideas and thinking)?

2. Consider the surprising importance of rules in children's play. How do the rules allow the play to continue?

3. Adolescents' imaginative play with fiction relies on rules, too. How do the rules of verisimilitude affect the play of story for the reader and the writer?

4. Discuss the following: "The writer finds that each word, linked to countless other words and meanings, strives to create its own coherence. Sometimes a battle for control ensues." Have you experienced this slippery linguistic play as you strive to translate your thoughts onto the page? How do you handle it?

5. What questions are you wondering about as you finish Chapter 1? Share them now with your colleagues or jot them down on a sticky note or two. We'll return to these questions again at the end of the book.

Chapter 2

Exercises That Stimulate Play, Engage Students, and Build Technique: Finding the Balance to Create Productive Fictional Worlds

1. The author offers three factors to consider for any writing exercise: play, technique, and scaffolding. Take a few moments to discuss each of these factors and to discuss what they mean in light of this book and also in your own experience as writers and teachers.

2. Apply the following scaffolding question in this chapter to your own classroom: What can my student writers do well with regard to fiction? What strengths do I find that I can build upon? Where will they need extra support?

3. Consider the revised Character Bags exercise. Would you use this exercise with your students? Why or why not? If so, what scaffolding would you add or remove for your students' particular needs?

4. Try the Dialogue-in-Scene activity or the Mad, Soft, and Fast Talking activity yourself. How did it feel to play with these ideas? What techniques did you sharpen? Share your writing with your group.

5. Do you have a favorite creative writing exercise? Share it with your group. Then, think about it in terms of play, technique, and scaffolding. See if you can identify why it is successful and also develop a few additional scaffolds that may help support students.

Chapter 3

Managing Play Through Revision

1. What problems do you encounter when you try to help students revise their writing? In what ways are your students similar to (or different from) the inexperienced writers discussed at the beginning of this chapter?

2. Discuss the difference between internal and external revisions. How might it be valuable to consider revision in two ways rather than as a single process?

3. Mary uses an artifact drawn from three students talking about titles as an example of a good way to get students talking about their process. How else might you get students reflecting about their writing? Brainstorm some possibilities.

4. After your next writing assignment, try asking your students to draw the writing process they used on that assignment. Have them share their drawings. Jot down some thoughts about what you see and learn from their responses.

5. Together with your colleagues, gather together the creative writing worksheets that are used in your school. Rethink the worksheets in terms of flexibility. Is there a way to reduce the number of questions asked or to allow students to customize their choices?

6. Now look at the worksheets in terms of timing. Can part of them be given prior to writing and the rest midway through the drafting process (or as part of revision)?

7. Discuss the possibilities for mixed-media revisions in your classroom—using sticky notes, track changes, or pen-and-scissors cutting and pasting. How might students' revision practices become more active, with more opportunities to play with possibilities for the developing text?

Chapter 4

Unprompted Writing: Learning How Writers Play

1. Discuss how students can learn to create their own ideas for writing, drawing from their own experience. In what ways is this beneficial for the students as writers and as adolescents?

2. As you read about the four teachers, which comes closest to your preferred teaching style? Or might you be a hybrid among the teachers? Why?

3. Which of the four vignettes—Kurt, John, Roxanne, or Denise—most surprised you? Why? What can be learned? Can you picture any of your students in these stories?

4. Take a few minutes to try Ms. Goodwin's topic search activity (in John's vignette). What stories, people, and events from your own life might make good subjects for fiction? Try drafting one into a paragraph—if it's working, keep going. Save every part of the process to share with students, so they can see how adult writers play, too.

5. How often have you experienced the use of clichéd images and expressions in student writing? Using the chapter and your colleagues as resources, look at ways to encourage students to *inhabit* their writing so that they do not rely on clichés in their fiction.

Chapter 5

Building a Creative Writing Curriculum

1. How do you conceive of your students in terms of writing: As creative thinkers? As teens who sometimes need a break from their focus on expository writing? As teens who may become lifelong writers (fiction and exposition)? How might this view help shape your curricular choices when teaching fiction?

2. The author identifies several characteristics of an effective writing curriculum. Which have you found most valuable in your teaching? Which would you like to develop further? Discuss potential ways to increase those characteristics. For example, how might you show students that you sanction imaginative play?

3. How do you use journals? Consider ways to tweak this so that students can use them to play like writers do—identifying and exploring ideas for writing.

4. What are the typical, daily features of your writing curriculum? Which of the suggested activities (e.g., writing time, student-generated questions, reflective writing, supportive exercises, and examining student writing for what works) do you already do? Which might you add or rotate in on a regular basis?

5. Take a look at the section called Supporting Play Throughout the Process. How might you tailor these ideas for your teaching style and your students? Identify a few elements to try out in the classroom. Then, report back to your colleagues and compare notes. Bring in some of the best student work to share.

6. How do you use peer feedback? Building on the ideas in the chapter, create a peer feedback form that your students can use.

7. Take some time to think about audience. How do your students celebrate and share their work? What other possibilities might there be to widen this audience?

Final Reflection

Look back at the questions you generated after Chapter 1. What answers have you found? (What questions remain?) As you continue to teach writing, invite as much reflection—your students, your colleagues, and your own—as you can. Use those ideas, and those in this book, to help you continue to create and refine spaces for *Writers at Play*.

Bibliography

Adler, Mary. 2007. "Playing with Fiction: Developing Adolescent Writers and Selves." *Journal of Teaching Writing* 23 (2): 23–34.

———. 2001. Play, Curriculum, and Narrative Writing Development: A Study of Four High School Creative Writing Classes. Dissertation. Albany: University at Albany, State University of New York.

Adler, Mary, and Eija Rougle. 2005. *Building Literacy through Classroom Discussion: Research-Based Strategies for Developing Critical Readers and Thoughtful Writers in Middle School.* New York: Scholastic.

Alvarez, Julia. 2002. Reader's Guide in *Before We Were Free,* pp. 169–78. New York: Random House.

Applebee, Arthur N. 1996. *Curriculum as Conversation: Transforming Traditions of Teaching and Learning.* Chicago: University of Chicago Press.

Arana, Marie, ed. 2003. *The Writing Life: Writers on How They Think and Work.* New York: PublicAffairs.

Atwell, Nancie. 1987. *In the Middle: Writing, Reading and Learning with Adolescents.* Portsmouth, NH: Heinemann.

Bakhtin, M. M. 1986. *Speech Genres and Other Late Essays.* Translated by Vern W. McGee. Austin: University of Texas Press.

Bereiter, Carl, and Marlene Scardamalia. 1987. *The Psychology of Written Composition.* Hillsdale, NJ: Lawrence Erlbaum.

Berk, Laura, Trisha Mann, and Amy Ogan. 2006. "Make-Believe Play: Wellspring for Development of Self-Regulation." In *Play= Learning: How Play Motivates and Enhances Children's Cognitive and Social-Emotional Growth*, edited by Dorothy Singer, Roberta Michnick Golinkoff, and Kathy Hirsh-Pasek, 74–100. Oxford, UK: Oxford University Press.

Bishop, Wendy. 1998. *Released into Language*. 2d ed. Portsmouth, NH: Boynton/Cook.

———. 1991. *Working Words*. Columbus, OH: McGraw-Hill.

Bruner, Jerome. 1990. "Culture and Human Development: A New Look." *Human Development* 33: 344–55.

Bruner, Jerome, Allison Jolly, and Kathy Sylva, eds. 1976. *Play: Its Role in Development and Evolution*. New York: Basic Books.

Butler, Robert Olen. 2005. *From Where You Dream: The Process of Writing Fiction*. New York: Grove Press.

Calkins, Lucy. 1986. *The Art of Teaching Writing*. Portsmouth, NH: Heinemann.

Chudacoff, Howard. 2007. *Children at Play: An American History*. New York: NYU Press.

Chukovsky, Kornei. 1963. *From Two to Five*. Translated by M. Morton. Berkeley, CA: University of California Press.

Csikszentmihayli, Mihalyi. 1979. "The Concept of Flow." In *Play and Learning*, edited by Brian Sutton-Smith, 257–74. New York: Gardner Press.

Daiute, Collette. 1990. "The Role of Play in Writing Development." *Research in the Teaching of English* 24 (1): 4–47.

———. 1986. "Physical and Cognitive Factors in the Revising Process: Insights from Studies with Computers." *Research in the Teaching of English* 20: 140–59.

Derrida, J. 1978. "Structure, Sign and Play in the Discourse of the Human Sciences." In *Writing and Difference*, edited by Jaques Derrida and translated by Alan Bass, 278–83. Chicago: University of Chicago Press.

Diamond, Adele. 2006. "The Early Development of Executive Functions." In *Lifespan Cognition: Mechanisms of Change*, edited by Ellen Bialystok and Fergus I. M. Craik, 70–95. Oxford, UK: Oxford University Press.

Diamond, Adele, W. Steven Barnett, Jessica Thomas, and Sarah Munro. 2007. "Preschool Program Improves Cognitive Control." *Science* 318: 1387–88.

Dix, Stephanie. 2006. "'What Did I Change and Why Did I Do It?': Young Writers' Revision Practices." *Literacy* 40 (1): 3–10.

Dyson, Anne Haas. 1997. *Writing Superheroes: Contemporary Childhood, Popular Culture, and Classroom Literacy.* New York: Teachers College Press.

———. 1993. *Social Worlds of Children Learning to Write in an Urban Primary School.* New York: Teachers College Press.

———. 1989. *Multiple Worlds of Child Writers: Friends Learning to Write.* New York: Teachers College Press.

Elbow, Peter. 1998. *Writing with Power.* 2d ed. Oxford, UK: Oxford University Press.

———. 1973. "The Doubting Game and the Believing Game." *Writing Without Teachers*, 147–91. Oxford, UK: Oxford University Press.

Ellis, Sherry. 2006. *Now Write!* New York: Penguin.

Emig, Janet. 1971. *The Composing Processes of Twelfth Graders.* Urbana, IL: National Council of Teachers of English.

Faigley, Lester, and Stephen Witte. 1981. "Analyzing Revision." *College Composition and Communication* 32 (4): 400–14.

Fitzgerald, Jill. 1987. "Research on Revision in Writing." *Review of Educational Research* 57 (4): 481–506.

Fletcher, Ralph. 1996. *A Writer's Notebook: Unlocking the Writer Within You.* New York: HarperCollins.

———. 1993. *What a Writer Needs.* Portsmouth, NH: Heinemann.

Flower, Linda, and John R. Hayes. 1981. "A Cognitive Process Theory of Writing." *College Composition and Communication* 32 (4): 365–387.

Freire, Paulo. 1997. *Pedagogy of Hope.* Granby, MA: Bergin & Garvey.

Gaiman, Neil. 2009. "Where Do You Get Your Ideas?" Accessed January 24, 2009 from www.neilgaiman.com/p/Cool_Stuff/Essays/Essays_By_Neil/Where_do_you_get_your_ideas%3F.

Gardner, John. 1984. *The Art of Fiction: Notes on Craft for Young Writers.* New York: Vintage.

Garvey, Catherine. 1990. *Play.* Enlarged ed. The Developing Child series, edited by Jerome Bruner, Michael Cole, and Annette Karmiloff-Smith. Cambridge, MA: Harvard University Press.

———. 1976. "Some Properties of Social Play." In *Play: Its Role in Development and Evolution,* edited by Jerome Bruner, 570–83. New York: Basic Books.

Gentile, Claudia A., James Martin-Rehrmann, and John H. Kennedy. 1995. "Windows into the Classroom: NAEP's 1992 Writing Portfolio Study." Washington, DC: National Center for Education Statistics.

Goldberg, Natalie. 1986. *Writing Down the Bones.* Boston: Shambhala.

Golinkoff, Roberta Michnick, Kathy Hirsch-Pasek, and Dorothy Singer. "Why Play=Learning: A Challenge for Parents and Educators." In *Play=Learning: How Play Motivates and Enhances Children's Cognitive and Social-Emotional Growth,* edited by Dorothy Singer, Roberta Michnick Golinkoff, and Kathy Hirsh-Pasek, 3–12. Oxford, UK: Oxford University Press.

Graves, Donald. 1989. *Experiment with Fiction: The Reading/Writing Teacher's Companion.* Portsmouth, NH: Heinemann.

———. 1983. *Writing: Teachers and Children at Work.* Portsmouth, NH: Heinemann.

Guare, John. 1992. "The Art of Theater IX: Interview with Anne Catteneo." *The Paris Review* 125: 69–103.

Hall, Nigel. 2000. "Literacy, Play, and Authentic Experience." In *Play and Literacy in Early Childhood,* edited by Kathy A. Roskos and James F. Christie, 189–204. Mahway, NJ: Lawrence Erlbaum.

Haneda, Mari, and Gordon Wells. 2000. "Writing in Knowledge-Building Communities." *Research in the Teaching of English* 34 (3): 430–57.

Heard, Georgia. 1998. *Awakening the Heart: Exploring Poetry in Elementary and Middle School.* Portsmouth, NH: Heinemann.

Hedegaard, Mariane. 2007. "The Development of Children's Conceptual Relation to the World, with a Focus on Concept Formation in Preschool Children's Activity." In *The Cambridge Companion to Vygotsky,* edited by Harry Daniels, Michael Cole, and James V. Wertsch, 246–75. Cambridge, UK: Cambridge University Press.

Herbert, Wray. 2008, June 4. "Is Ef the New Iq?" *Newsweek.* Accessed January 30, 2009 at www.newsweek.com/id/139885.

Hillocks, George Jr. 2002. *The Testing Trap: How State Writing Assessments Control Learning.* New York Teachers College Press.

Holmes, Vicki, and Margaret Moulton. 1994. "The Writing Process in Multicultural Settings." *Journal of Reading* 37 (8): 628–34.

Jaffrey, Zia. 2000. "Toni Morrison: The Salon Interview." Accessed March 31, 2009 at www.salon.com/books/int/1998/02/cov_si_02int.html.

Kirby, Dan, Tom Liner, and Ruth Vinz. 1988. *Inside Out.* 2d ed. Portsmouth, NH: Boynton/Cook.

Kittle, Penny. 2008. *Write Beside Them.* Portsmouth, NH: Heinemann.

Krischenblatt-Gimblett, Barbara. 1979. "Speech Play and Verbal Art." In *Play and Learning,* edited by Brian Sutton-Smith, 219–38. New York: Gardner Press.

Lamott, Anne. 1994. *Bird by Bird.* New York: Random House.

Langer, Judith. 1995. *Envisioning Literature: Literary Understanding and Literature Instruction.* New York: Teachers College Press.

LeGuin, Ursula K. 1998. *Steering the Craft.* Portland, OR: Eighth Mountain Press.

Lillard, Angeline. 2001. "Pretend Play as Twin Earth: A Social-Cognitive Analysis." *Developmental Review* 21: 495–531.

Lonergan, Kenneth. 2000. *You Can Count on Me.* Shooting draft of screenplay. The Weekly Script: Movie Script Archive. Accessed May 11, 2009 at www.weeklyscript.com.

Madison, Deborah. 1997. *Vegetarian Cooking for Everyone.* New York: Broadway Books.

McCaffrey, Larry. 1996. *Some Other Frequency: Interviews with Innovative American Authors.* Philadelphia: University of Pennsylvania Press.

McCaffrey, Larry, and Sinda Gregory, eds. 1987. *Alive and Writing: Interview with American Authors of the 1980s.* Urbana, IL: University of Illinois Press.

Minot, Stephen. 1998. *Three Genres: The Writing of Poetry, Fiction, and Drama.* 6th ed. Upper Saddle River, NJ: Prentice Hall.

Murray, Donald M. 1989. "Unlearning to Write." In *Creative Writing in America,* edited by Joseph M. Moxley, 103–14. Urbana, IL: National Council of Teachers of English.

Neel, Jasper. 1988. *Plato, Derrida, and Writing.* Carbondale, IL: Southern Illinois University Press.

Newkirk, Thomas. 1997. *The Performance of Self in Student Writing.* Portsmouth, NH: Boynton/Cook.

Paley, Vivian Gussin. 1991. *Bad Guys Don't Have Birthdays.* Chicago: University of Chicago Press.

Perl, Sandra. 1979. "The Composing Processes of Unskilled College Writers." *Research in the Teaching of English* 13: 317–36.

Pink, Daniel. 2005. *A Whole New Mind: Moving from the Information Age to the Conceptual Age.* New York: Penguin.

Quintero, Elizabeth P. 2009. *Critical Literacy in Early Childhood Education: Artful Story and the Integrated Curriculum.* New York: Peter Lang.

Rabinovitch, Dina. 2003. "His Bright Materials: Interview with Philip Pullman." Accessed March 31, 2009 at www.guardian.co.uk/ books/2003/dec/10/booksforchildrenandteenagers.familyand relationships1. Or at www.philip-pullman.com/pages/content/ index.asp?PageID=118.

Rief, Linda. 2007. "Writing: Commonsense Matters." In *Adolescent Literacy: Turning Promise into Practice,* edited by Kylene Beers, Robert Probst, and Linda Rief. Portsmouth, NH: Heinemann.

Robbins, Tom. 1987. In *Alive and Writing: Interview with American Authors of the 1980s,* edited by Larry McCaffrey and Sinda Gregory. Urbana, IL: University of Illinois Press.

Rogoff, Barbara. 1990. *Apprenticeship in Thinking: Cognitive Development in Social Context.* New York: Oxford University Press.

Romano, Tom. 2007. "Teaching Writing from the Inside." In *Adolescent Literacy: Turning Promise into Practice,* edited by Kylene Beers, Robert Probst, and Linda Rief. Portsmouth, NH: Heinemann.

Rule, Rebecca, and Susan Wheeler. 1993. *Creating the Story*. Portsmouth, NH: Heinemann.

Sebranek, Patrick, Dave Kemper, and Verne Meyer, eds. 2006. *Writers INC*. Wilmington, MA: Great Source.

Smith, Patricia. 2008. Interview broadcast November 9 in a segment titled *Poetry Instead* on the Wisconsin Public Radio program, *To the Best of Our Knowledge*. Wisconsin Public Radio. Program 08-11-09. Retrieved February 20, 2009 from www.wpr.org/book/081109a.cfm.

Sommers, Nancy. 1980. "Revision Strategies of Student Writers and Experienced Adult Writers." *College Composition and Communication* 31: 378–88.

U.S. Department of Education. 2003. Institute of Education Sciences. National Center for Education Statistics. The Nation's Report Card: Writing 2002, NCES 2003–529, by H. R. Persky, M. C. Daane, and Y. Jin. Washington, DC: U.S. Department of Education.

Valentine, Vikki. 2008. "Your Health Q&A: The Best Kind of Play for Kids." Accessed March 31, 2009 at www.npr.org/templates/story/story.php?storyId=73598288.

Vanderberg, Robert, and H. Lee Swanson. 2007. "Which Components of Working Memory Are Important in the Writing Process?" *Reading and Writing: An Interdisciplinary Journal* 20 (7): 721–52.

Vygotsky, Lev. 1978. *Mind and Society*. Cambridge, MA: Harvard University Press.

Yagelski, Robert. 1995. "The Role of Classroom Context in the Revision Strategies of Student Writers." *Research in the Teaching of English* 29 (2): 216–238.